Contents

Easy-Freeze

INSTANT POT PRESSURE COOKER

COOKBOOK

100 Freeze-Ahead, Make-in-Minutes Recipes
for Every Multi-Cooker

ELLA SANDERS

CASTLE POINT BOOKS
NEW YORK

www.castlepointbooks.com
www.stmartins.com

The Castle Point Books trademark is owned by Castle Point Publishing, LLC.
Castle Point books are published and distributed by St. Martin's Press.
ISBN 978-1-250-18188-6 (trade paperback)

Production Design by Mary Velgos
Cover and interior images used by permission from Shutterstock.com

Our books may be purchased in bulk for promotional, educational, or business
use. Please contact your local bookseller or the Macmillan Corporate and
Premium Sales Department at 1-800-221-7945, extension 5442,
or by email at MacmillanSpecialMarkets@macmillan.com.

Instant Pot is a registered trademark of Double Insight Inc. *The Easy-Freeze
Instant Pot Pressure Cooker Cookbook* is an independently created book and
is not endorsed, sponsored, or authorized by Double Insight Inc.

First Edition: August 2018

10 9 8 7 6 5 4 3 2 1

Introduction

YOU'VE GOT THIS DINNER THING IN THE BAG. LITERALLY.
Who doesn't want to come home after a long day and not have to worry about what's for dinner? Too often the modern evening meal can seem like one challenge too many, and it's easier to fall back on the delivery routine, heat up a frozen pizza, or simply eat out more often than you (and your budget) would like. If that sounds like your life, and you're looking for a new way to get a home-cooked meal on the table every night for your family, then *Easy-Freeze Instant Pot Pressure Cooker Cookbook* may be just what you're looking for.

Electric pressure cookers have revolutionized cooking in the last few years. It's now possible to contemplate dishes like pot roasts, long-simmering stews, and even ribs on a weeknight. And given that you don't have to do anything to the pot while it's cooking, it's become a godsend for multitaskers who need to help kids with homework, return emails, and catch up on household chores—all while making a home-cooked meal.

With *Easy-Freeze Instant Pot Pressure Cooker Cookbook*, this convenience factor is taken to the next level with dozens of simple recipes you prep in advance, freeze, and then pop into your multi-cooker when you're ready to eat. You choose how many meals you want to make in advance—a week's or even a month's worth!—and dedicate a few hours or more on a weekend to preparing, bagging, and freezing the ingredients. It's fun, easy, and even something you can do together as a family, because most of the work involves simple chopping and measuring. On serving day, you add some liquid to your pot—usually in the form of flavor-building stock—place the frozen meal into the multi-cooker, and pressure-cook it until done. It's almost as easy as a TV dinner or takeout, but infinitely better because you make it yourself and can choose ingredients that are good for your family. In a time when we're becoming more conscious about food waste, this method wastes less food because you buy only what you need, prep it, and freeze it. It doesn't have time to languish and spoil in the fridge only to be tossed away. You may also find that it saves you money because you're sticking to your shopping list!

With the Easy-Freeze method, you'll always know the answer to the question: *What's for dinner?*

HOW TO EASY-FREEZE

With one day of big effort and a minimum of weeknight effort, Easy-Freeze helps you win the weeknight. First, choose the recipes you want to make. Then, make a list, checking to see what you've already got on hand and what you need to buy. Next, head to the store and shop! If you're preparing a week's worth of food, you can shop in the morning and do the prep work in the afternoon, but if you're doing two or more weeks, you may want to shop the day before so you can start the following morning. Finally, it's time to roll up your sleeves, clear the countertops, and prep!

Many of these recipes use the same cuts of meat: boneless, skinless chicken thighs; chuck roast; pork shoulder; etc. There are several reasons for that. First, you can take advantage of larger, more economical packages, such as those you might find at a warehouse club or a family pack at your supermarket. Also, these cuts tend to be a little less expensive. Most importantly, though, these cuts are the best fit for pressure cooking. Lean cuts like chicken breast and pork tenderloin can dry out too easily, leading to disappointment.

Some recipes require you to add a few ingredients on cooking day, namely perishable items that don't freeze or pressure-cook well (for example, dairy, some herbs, and vegetables that are meant to stay crunchy). If you're preparing a week's worth of meals, you may want to pick up all of these serving-day items at once to have on hand. For two or more weeks, it's better to buy the items later to avoid spoilage.

To speed the prep work, you can chop onions and other vegetables in a food processor, and no one will be the wiser if you use pre-minced garlic. (Hint: If you do, a teaspoon of minced garlic is about one clove, so a tablespoon would be about three cloves.) If you're very pressed for time, you can even buy precut veggies! If you're making several recipes that require you to precook ground beef or turkey, you can cook all of the meat at once, and then divide it up as needed for the recipes. To make the meats freezer and multi-cooker friendly, they're chopped into chunks. That way, they'll cook evenly, and you won't be left with something that's overcooked on the outside and still frozen in the center.

Once you've prepped your ingredients, you'll place them in gallon-size freezer bags, label, and seal them. Then you'll put the bags in round containers so that they freeze into a round shape that can be put directly in the multi-cooker. (If you're having a hard time releasing the frozen food from the plastic bag, you can run it under warm water for a minute or two and it should slide right out.)

On serving day, you'll need to add liquid in order for the multi-cooker to come up to pressure. Most models need about a cup of liquid, but check your manual to see what your machine's particular requirements are and increase the liquid if necessary. To build flavor, the recipes in this book generally call for stock (chicken, beef, or vegetable). In a pinch, you can use water, but you may want to taste and adjust the seasonings at the end to compensate. On pages 10–12, you'll find tasty recipes for homemade stock, but it's perfectly fine to use canned stock or a concentrated chicken, beef, or vegetable base in water. If you use frozen homemade stock, just add it to the multi-cooker first, set it on Sauté, and once it has melted, add your food and proceed with the recipe.

What You'll Need

Gallon-size freezer bags. You'll put your prep ingredients in these bags.

Round freezer-safe containers (7-inch diameter). Because you'll be putting the frozen ingredients in the multi-cooker, you'll need to make sure the items will fit! By placing your sealed prep bag inside a round container, you'll ensure the items freeze in the shape you need. If you freeze the items flat, you'll never get them in the pot! Once the food is frozen, you can remove it from the container.

Instant-read thermometer. After cooking, it's very important to take readings in several different spots to make sure the food is thoroughly cooked and there are no cold spots.

Silicone baking mitt(s). Wear these when releasing the pressure valve to protect yourself from the steam. They're also useful when removing the inner pot.

A 6- or 7-inch springform pan or baking pan with removable bottom is needed if you plan to make lasagna.

Marker or labels. Don't forget to label your prep bags with the name of the dish. It may be helpful to add the page number of the recipe, so you can quickly and easily find the serving day directions.

The multi-cooker will take longer to come up to pressure than you're used to, sometimes 20 minutes or longer, because the food thaws out before it's cooked.

TROUBLESHOOTING

Too much liquid. Pressure cookers require a certain amount of liquid to come up to pressure. The amount varies by model, but it's generally between 1 and 2 cups. In addition, the cooking method itself forces foods to release a lot of their liquid, and unlike stovetop cooking, not much of that liquid is lost through evaporation. This means that when you open the lid, there may be a lot more liquid in the pot than you were expecting. To reduce your sauce and concentrate its flavor, simmer the liquid for a few minutes until it reaches the desired consistency. If your dish includes a meat that can be easily overcooked, remove it to a plate before you reduce the sauce. You can also mix together a tablespoon of cornstarch with enough water to dissolve, stir it into the pot, and simmer for a few minutes until the sauce has thickened.

The pot won't come up to pressure. Because the food is frozen, it can take 20 minutes or more to defrost and come to pressure. But if it doesn't come up to pressure, check to make sure that the steam release handle has been switched to "sealing" and that you've included enough liquid.

Something other than steam comes out of the steam release handle. Return the handle to the sealing position and allow the pressure to release naturally. It's possible that foam has built up inside the pot or that the pot is overfilled. Be sure to clean it thoroughly afterward to avoid any blockages. Certain foods, such as oatmeal and other starchy or dehydrated items, require a natural release. Refer to your owner's manual for more information.

Smelly silicone sealing ring. The silicone ring tends to absorb cooking odors. Remove and wash it after every use, and let it dry thoroughly. If you are particularly bothered by the smell, you can use a separate ring for sweet and savory dishes.

The timer starts counting down and the pot has not yet come to pressure. There is most likely not enough liquid. Open the pot, stir, add a bit more liquid, and try again.

Food is still frozen. There are variations by pot and by manufacturer, so your meals could take a little more or less than the stated time. If you open the pot and find that part of the food is still frozen, use a wooden spoon to break up the frozen section and stir well. You can either return it to pressure for a few minutes, or if it is almost done, just simmer with the lid off until it is cooked through.

The Basics

Makes 6 cups

Prep time
10 minutes

Pressure time
30 minutes

Release method
Natural

Chicken Stock

While it's perfectly fine to use canned chicken stock or broth in the recipes in this book, homemade stock tastes so much better, and it's surprisingly simple to make. You control both the quality of the ingredients and the amount of salt that gets added. Don't skip the important step of refrigerating the stock before freezing it. The fat will rise to the surface, so you can just skim it off.

PREP INGREDIENTS

2 pounds chicken wings, split

1 onion, halved

2 carrots, cut into 2 or 3 pieces

2 ribs celery, cut into 2 or 3 pieces

2 sprigs thyme

2 sprigs parsley

1 bay leaf

½ teaspoon whole peppercorns

1 teaspoon vinegar

Salt to taste

PREP DIRECTIONS

Place all the ingredients in the multi-cooker inner pot. Add 6 cups water, being sure not to fill the pot more than two-thirds full. Cook on high pressure for 30 minutes, and then let the pressure release naturally. When cool enough to handle, strain the stock into a storage container and refrigerate until cold. Skim any fat from the surface. Portion into ½-cup or 1-cup servings and freeze.

Beef Stock

Roasting the short ribs or soup bones helps make a richer, more deeply flavored beef stock. If you use soup bones, choose meaty ones. Keep an eye on the liquid level in the multi-cooker, and don't go over two-thirds full. If you need to, you can always use a little bit less water.

Makes 6 cups

Prep time
10 minutes

Pressure time
60 minutes

Release method
Natural

PREP INGREDIENTS

3 pounds bone-in beef short ribs or beef soup bones

2 tablespoons olive oil

Salt and pepper to taste

1 onion, halved

2 carrots, cut into 2 or 3 pieces

2 ribs celery, cut into 2 or 3 pieces

2 sprigs thyme

½ bunch parsley

1 bay leaf

2 teaspoons whole peppercorns

1 teaspoon vinegar

PREP DIRECTIONS

Preheat the oven to 400°F. Rub the ribs with the oil, season with salt and pepper, and place on a sheet pan. Transfer the sheet pan to the oven and roast for 30 minutes. Place the roasted ribs and the remaining ingredients in the multi-cooker. Add 6 cups water, being sure not to fill the pot more than two-thirds full. Cook on high pressure for 60 minutes, and then let the pressure release naturally. When cool enough to handle, strain the stock into a storage container and refrigerate until cold. Skim any fat from the surface. Portion into ½-cup or 1-cup servings and freeze.

Makes 6 cups

Prep time
10 minutes

Pressure time
20 minutes

Release method
Natural

Vegetable Stock

In the absence of meat, dried mushrooms and a splash of soy sauce will help boost the savory, umami flavor in this simple vegetable stock. If you don't have or can't find parsnips, you can substitute a potato.

PREP INGREDIENTS

2 leeks, well cleaned and cut into a few pieces

2 carrots, cut into 2 or 3 pieces

2 ribs celery, cut into 2 or 3 pieces

2 parsnips, cut into a few pieces

2 dried shiitake or porcini mushrooms

2 sprigs thyme

½ bunch parsley

1 bay leaf

2 tablespoons olive oil

1 tablespoon soy sauce

½ teaspoon whole black peppercorns

Salt to taste

PREP DIRECTIONS

Place all the ingredients in the multi-cooker inner pot. Add 6 cups water, being sure not to fill the pot more than two-thirds full. Cook on high pressure for 20 minutes, and then let the pressure release naturally. When cool, strain, portion into ½-cup or 1-cup servings and freeze.

Soups

Serves 4

Prep time
5 minutes

Pressure time
5 minutes

Release method
Natural (10 minutes)

Chicken, Corn, and Rice Soup

Chicken, Corn, and Rice Soup is a great way to use up leftover roasted chicken, and because it includes ingredients you're likely to have around the house, it's easy to throw together and keep in the freezer for a day when you or a family member is feeling a little under the weather. You can add in a big handful of chopped parsley at the end, or if you're in the mood for noodles, toss them in the soup after pressure cooking and let them simmer away until tender.

PREP INGREDIENTS

2 cups cooked chicken, cut into bite-size pieces

2 tablespoons olive oil

½ onion, finely chopped

1 carrot, peeled and finely chopped

1 rib celery, chopped

Salt and pepper to taste

1 cup frozen corn

SERVING DAY INGREDIENTS

3 cups chicken stock

¼ cup long-grain white rice

PREP DIRECTIONS

Combine all the prep ingredients in a 1-gallon resealable freezer bag. Squeeze out the air, label, and place in a round container to freeze into shape.

SERVING DAY DIRECTIONS

Add the chicken stock, the rice, and the contents of the package to the multi-cooker inner pot. Cook on high pressure for 5 minutes. Let the pressure release naturally for 10 minutes, and then manually release any remaining pressure.

Tortilla Soup

Tortilla Soup is like a party in a bowl: tender bites of chicken, crunchy strips of fried tortilla, and creamy avocado chunks all in a rich tomato- and cumin-spiked broth. Jarred salsa is your shortcut to big flavor fast. Serve with corn chips or crushed tortilla chips, shredded Monterey Jack cheese, jalapeño slices (fresh or pickled), diced avocado, chopped cilantro, and sour cream.

Serves 4

Prep time
10 minutes

Pressure time
8 minutes

Release method
Natural (10 minutes)

PREP INGREDIENTS

1 pound boneless, skinless chicken thighs, cut into 1½-inch chunks

1 (15.5-ounce) can black beans, drained and rinsed

1 (16-ounce) jar salsa

2 tablespoons tomato paste

1 tablespoon olive oil

½ cup frozen corn

1 onion, chopped

3 cloves garlic, minced

2 teaspoons ground cumin

1 teaspoon paprika

1 teaspoon dried oregano

Salt and pepper to taste

SERVING DAY INGREDIENTS

2½ cups chicken stock

PREP DIRECTIONS

Combine all the prep ingredients in a 1-gallon resealable freezer bag. Squeeze out the air, label, and place in a round container to freeze into shape.

SERVING DAY DIRECTIONS

Add the stock and the contents of the package to the multi-cooker inner pot. Cook on high pressure for 8 minutes. Let the pressure release naturally for 10 minutes, and then manually release any remaining pressure. Serve with any or all of the suggested toppings (see headnote).

Serves 4 to 6

Prep time
15 minutes

Pressure time
5 minutes

Release method
Natural (10 minutes)

Classic Ham and Bean Soup

Hearty, comforting, and delicious, Classic Ham and Bean Soup is big on flavor and easy on effort. Don't be tempted to add salt to the soup until after it's finished. You'll likely find that between the ham and the stock, it's perfectly seasoned as is. White pepper has floral, earthy notes, but if you don't have it on hand, just substitute regular black pepper.

PREP INGREDIENTS

1 large potato, peeled and cubed (optional)

2 (15.5-ounce) cans Great Northern or cannellini beans, drained and rinsed

½ pound ham steak, cubed

1 small onion, chopped

1 carrot, sliced into ½-inch rounds

1 rib celery, sliced

¼ teaspoon white pepper

½ teaspoon dried marjoram or ¼ teaspoon dried rosemary

1 cup chicken broth

SERVING DAY INGREDIENTS

2 cups chicken stock

PREP DIRECTIONS

If using the potato, bring a large pot of salted water to a boil over high heat. Add the potato and blanch for 2 to 3 minutes. Drain and set aside in a single layer to cool. (A kitchen towel is useful for this task.) Add the potatoes and the remaining prep ingredients to a 1-gallon resealable freezer bag. Squeeze out the air, label, and place in a round container to freeze into shape.

SERVING DAY DIRECTIONS

Add the chicken stock and the contents of the package to the multi-cooker inner pot. Cook on high pressure for 5 minutes. Let the pressure release naturally for 10 minutes, and then manually release any remaining pressure.

Corn Chowder

Simple and satisfying, Corn Chowder has a secret ingredient: canned green chiles. While they don't add much in the way of heat, they do add tons of flavor. On cooking day, just fry up a few slices of bacon until crispy and crumble a slice on top of each bowl along with some chopped parsley or chives.

Serves 4

Prep time
10 minutes

Pressure time
5 minutes

Release method
Natural (10 minutes)

PREP INGREDIENTS

1 (14.75-ounce) can cream-style corn

1 (12-ounce) package frozen corn

1 onion, chopped

1 carrot, finely chopped

1 (4.5-ounce) can green chiles

1 teaspoon garlic powder

Salt and pepper to taste

SERVING DAY INGREDIENTS

2 cups chicken or vegetable stock

¼ cup instant potato flakes

1 cup whole milk or half-and-half

2 tablespoons unsalted butter

PREP DIRECTIONS

Combine all the prep ingredients in a 1-gallon resealable freezer bag. Squeeze out the air, label, and place in a round container to freeze into shape.

SERVING DAY DIRECTIONS

Add the stock and the contents of the package to the multi-cooker inner pot. Cook on high pressure for 5 minutes. Let the pressure release naturally for 10 minutes, and then manually release any remaining pressure. Stir in the potato flakes, milk, and butter.

Serves 4

Prep time
10 minutes

Pressure time
5 minutes

Release method
Natural (5 minutes)

Broccoli Cheddar Soup

Broccoli Cheddar Soup is so delicious but you might have thought it too difficult to make at home. Not so! Now you can have it whenever the craving strikes. Serve with crusty bread, or better yet, in bread bowls!

PREP INGREDIENTS

1 pound broccoli, cut into bite-size pieces, stems peeled and thinly sliced

½ onion, minced or grated

1 carrot, shredded

2 cloves garlic, minced

1 cup chicken or vegetable stock

1 teaspoon mustard powder

Salt and pepper to taste

SERVING DAY INGREDIENTS

1 cup chicken or vegetable stock

4 ounces (about 1 cup) shredded cheddar cheese

2 tablespoons unsalted butter

½ cup heavy cream or half-and-half

PREP DIRECTIONS

Combine all the prep ingredients in a 1-gallon resealable freezer bag. Squeeze out the air, label, and place in a round container to freeze into shape.

SERVING DAY DIRECTIONS

Add the stock and the contents of the package to the multi-cooker inner pot. Cook on high pressure for 5 minutes. Let the pressure release naturally for 5 minutes, and then manually release any remaining pressure. Gradually stir in the cheddar cheese, butter, and heavy cream until the cheese is melted. Using an immersion blender, puree the soup.

Serves 4

Prep time
10 minutes

Pressure time
5 minutes

Release method
Natural (10 minutes)

Creamy Roasted Tomato and Basil Soup

By using canned fire-roasted tomatoes, you can get a delicious roasted flavor without any of the effort. To make this soup lighter, leave out the cream and butter and just drizzle a little extra-virgin olive oil in each bowl at the end. Serve Creamy Roasted Tomato and Basil Soup with grilled cheese sandwiches, of course.

PREP INGREDIENTS

1 (28-ounce) can crushed
fire-roasted tomatoes

1 small onion, chopped

3 cloves garlic, minced

½ cup packed fresh basil leaves

1 teaspoon sugar

Salt and pepper to taste

Pinch crushed red pepper flakes (optional)

SERVING DAY INGREDIENTS

1½ cups chicken stock

¾ cup heavy cream

2 tablespoons unsalted butter

¼ cup thinly sliced fresh basil

PREP DIRECTIONS

Combine all the prep ingredients in a 1-gallon resealable freezer bag. Squeeze out the air, label, and place in a round container to freeze into shape.

SERVING DAY DIRECTIONS

Add the stock and the contents of the package to the multi-cooker inner pot. Cook on high pressure for 5 minutes. Let the pressure release naturally for 10 minutes, and then manually release any remaining pressure. Stir in the heavy cream, butter, and fresh basil.

Lentil Kale Soup

Lentil Kale Soup is healthy, delicious, and hearty enough to be a meal. Even if you're not a fan of kale, you might find yourself changing your mind, as the kale turns meltingly tender in this soup. If you wish, you can also add some diced ham to the prep ingredients; just cut back on the salt. Prep tip: If you're making a number of meals at once, start your lentils at the beginning of the day, so they're cooked and cooled by the time you're assembling your bags.

Serves 4

Prep time
15 minutes

Pressure time
7 minutes

Release method
Natural (10 minutes)

PREP INGREDIENTS

1 cup dried brown lentils, picked over for debris and rinsed

3 cups chopped fresh kale (stems removed)

1 onion, chopped

1 carrot, chopped

1 rib celery, chopped

½ teaspoon dried thyme

½ teaspoon dried marjoram or oregano

1 bay leaf

2 tablespoons tomato paste

2 tablespoons olive oil

Salt and pepper to taste

SERVING DAY INGREDIENTS

2 cups vegetable stock

¼ cup chopped fresh parsley (optional)

2 teaspoons red or white wine vinegar

Extra-virgin olive oil, for drizzling

PREP DIRECTIONS

Add the lentils to the multi-cooker along with enough water to cover by about 2 inches. Lock the lid and cook on high pressure for 10 minutes. Let the pressure release naturally and drain the lentils, reserving 1 cup of the cooking water. It's okay if the lentils are still a bit firm; they'll finish cooking in the soup. Once the lentils are cool, add them, the reserved cooking water, and the remaining prep ingredients to a 1-gallon resealable freezer bag. Squeeze out the air, label, and place in a round container to freeze into shape.

SERVING DAY DIRECTIONS

Add the stock and the contents of the package to the multi-cooker inner pot. Cook on high pressure for 7 minutes. Let the pressure release naturally for 10 minutes, and then manually release any remaining pressure. Remove and discard the bay leaf. Stir in the parsley (if using) and the vinegar, and drizzle with extra-virgin olive oil.

Asian Chicken Noodle Soup

With fragrant ginger, savory shiitakes, and crunchy fresh vegetables, this noodle soup has a lot to love. You can vary the vegetable combination depending on what you have on hand or what's in season, and you can even stir in some cubed tofu for extra protein. Look for fresh udon noodles in the refrigerated case of your supermarket. If you can only find the kind that comes with a seasoning packet, just discard the packet and use the noodles.

Serves 4 to 6

Prep time
10 minutes

Pressure time
7 minutes

Release method
Natural (5 minutes)

PREP INGREDIENTS

1 pound boneless, skinless chicken thighs, cut into 1½-inch chunks

1 carrot, sliced into rounds

3 or 4 dried shiitake mushrooms

1 jalapeño or serrano chile, thinly sliced (optional)

1 tablespoon chopped fresh ginger

¼ cup soy sauce

1 tablespoon brown sugar

1 tablespoon rice vinegar

SERVING DAY INGREDIENTS

3 cups chicken stock

8 ounces fresh udon noodles

1 teaspoon sesame oil

1 cup green beans, cut into thirds, or snow peas (optional)

A few handfuls of torn bok choy leaves

Bean sprouts, for garnish

Sliced green onions, for garnish

PREP DIRECTIONS

Combine all the prep ingredients in a 1-gallon resealable freezer bag. Squeeze out the air, label, and place in a round container to freeze into shape.

SERVING DAY DIRECTIONS

Add the stock and the contents of the package to the multi-cooker inner pot. Cook on high pressure for 7 minutes. Let the pressure release naturally for 5 minutes, and then manually release any remaining pressure. Carefully remove the mushrooms and thinly slice them. Return them to the pot along with the udon noodles and sesame oil. If desired, stir in the green beans, add the bok choy, and garnish with bean sprouts and green onion. Let stand for a few minutes until the noodles are heated through and the vegetables are slightly cooked but still crunchy.

Serves 4 to 6

Prep time
10 minutes

Pressure time
8 minutes

Release method
Natural (8 minutes)

Butternut Squash and Sage Soup

Sweet butternut squash and woodsy sage make this simple soup comforting and inviting on an autumn evening. For a little crunch, garnish each bowl with a few pumpkin seeds.

PREP INGREDIENTS

1 (3- to 4-pound) butternut squash, peeled, seeded, and cut into 1-inch cubes

1 onion, chopped

2 cloves garlic, minced

2 tablespoons chopped fresh sage

1 cup vegetable or chicken stock

Salt and pepper to taste

SERVING DAY INGREDIENTS

2 cups vegetable or chicken stock

3 tablespoons unsalted butter

½ cup heavy cream (optional)

PREP DIRECTIONS

Combine all the prep ingredients in a 1-gallon resealable freezer bag. Squeeze out the air, label, and place in a round container to freeze into shape.

SERVING DAY DIRECTIONS

Add the stock and the contents of the package to the multi-cooker inner pot. Cook on high pressure for 8 minutes, and then let the pressure release naturally. Stir in the butter and heavy cream (if desired). Use an immersion blender to puree the soup.

Serves 4 to 6

Prep time
15 minutes

Pressure time
5 minutes

Release method
Natural (10 minutes)

Pesto Minestrone Soup

Pesto isn't just for pasta and chicken. Here it gives amazing flavor to this Pesto Minestrone Soup. If you wish, while the soup is cooking, you can cook 1 cup ditalini pasta on the stovetop and stir it into the soup when it's finished. If desired, serve with an additional dollop of pesto, a sprinkle of grated Parmesan cheese, and a drizzle of extra-virgin olive oil.

PREP INGREDIENTS

1 large Yukon gold potato, peeled and cubed

2 tablespoons olive oil

1 onion, chopped

1 carrot, sliced into rounds

¼ small head green cabbage, sliced

1 zucchini, chopped

1 cup frozen green beans

1 (15.5-ounce) can cannellini or Great Northern beans, drained and rinsed

½ cup canned diced tomatoes

1 cup vegetable or chicken stock

¼ cup prepared pesto sauce

Salt and pepper to taste

SERVING DAY INGREDIENTS

2 cups vegetable or chicken stock

PREP DIRECTIONS

Bring a large pot of salted water to a boil over high heat. Add the potatoes and blanch for 2 to 3 minutes. Drain and set aside in a single layer to cool. (A kitchen towel is useful for this task.) Combine the cooled potatoes and the remaining prep ingredients in a 1-gallon resealable freezer bag. Squeeze out the air, label, and place in a round container to freeze into shape.

SERVING DAY DIRECTIONS

Add the stock and the contents of the package to the multi-cooker inner pot. Cook on high pressure for 5 minutes. Let the pressure release naturally for 10 minutes, and then release any remaining pressure.

Potato Leek Soup

This classic soup is a wonderful example of how just a few humble ingredients, like potatoes and leeks, can combine to make something incredibly satisfying. The blanching step may seem a little fussy, but it prevents the potatoes from turning grainy in the freezer. For a richer version, stir in ½ cup heavy cream or half-and-half after the soup is done cooking.

Serves 4

Prep time
15 minutes

Pressure time
8 minutes

Release method
Natural

PREP INGREDIENTS

4 medium red or Yukon gold potatoes, peeled and cubed

3 large leeks, white part only, well cleaned and sliced

2 tablespoons unsalted butter

2 tablespoons chopped fresh parsley

¼ teaspoon ground thyme

1 cup chicken or vegetable stock

Salt and pepper to taste

SERVING DAY INGREDIENTS

1½ cups chicken or vegetable stock

PREP DIRECTIONS

Bring a large pot of salted water to a boil over high heat. Add the potatoes and blanch for 2 to 3 minutes. Drain and set aside in a single layer to cool. (A kitchen towel is useful for this task.) Combine the cooled potatoes with the remaining prep ingredients in a 1-gallon resealable freezer bag. Squeeze out the air, label, and place in a round container to freeze into shape.

SERVING DAY DIRECTIONS

Add the stock and the contents of the package to the multi-cooker inner pot. Cook on high pressure for 8 minutes, and then let the pressure release naturally. If desired, use an immersion blender to puree the soup.

Serves 4 to 6

Prep time
10 minutes

Pressure time
15 minutes

Release method
Natural

Split Pea and Ham Soup

With today's multi-cookers, you can make split pea soup without fear that it will end up on the ceiling! This simple version is filling enough for a meal with some crusty bread or cornbread and a salad.

PREP INGREDIENTS

1 pound dried green split peas, picked over for debris and rinsed

1 onion, chopped

2 ribs celery, chopped

1 teaspoon ground thyme

½ pound ham steak, finely chopped

Salt and pepper to taste

SERVING DAY INGREDIENTS

4 cups chicken or vegetable stock

4 strips bacon (optional)

Sour cream, for garnish (optional)

PREP DIRECTIONS

Combine all the prep ingredients in a 1-gallon resealable freezer bag. Squeeze out the air, label, and place in a round container to freeze into shape.

SERVING DAY DIRECTIONS

Add the stock and the contents of the package to the multi-cooker inner pot. Cook on high pressure for 15 minutes, and then let the pressure release naturally. Meanwhile, if desired, cook the bacon in a skillet until crispy. Transfer to a paper towel-lined plate to drain. Crumble the bacon over the soup and serve with dollops of sour cream.

Greens and Beans Soup

In addition to being a tasty way to get your veggies, Greens and Beans Soup is deliciously complex thanks to the addition of a smoked turkey wing. A big handful of chopped parsley at the end provides a burst of nutrients like vitamins A and C.

Serves 2

Prep time
10 minutes

Pressure time
5 minutes

Release method
Natural

PREP INGREDIENTS

1 smoked turkey wing, meat removed and torn into bite-size pieces

1 (15.5-ounce) can cannellini or small white beans, drained and rinsed

1 onion, chopped

2 cloves garlic, chopped

8 ounces frozen collard greens

1 bay leaf

Salt and pepper to taste

SERVING DAY INGREDIENTS

2 cups chicken or vegetable stock

¼ cup chopped fresh parsley (optional)

PREP DIRECTIONS

Combine all the prep ingredients in a 1-gallon resealable freezer bag. Squeeze out the air, label, and place in a round container to freeze into shape.

SERVING DAY DIRECTIONS

Add the stock and the contents of the package to the multi-cooker inner pot. Cook on high pressure for 5 minutes, and then let the pressure release naturally. Remove the bay leaf. If desired, stir in the fresh parsley.

Vegetable Beef Soup

Almost as easy as opening a can, but infinitely tastier, Vegetable Beef Soup is sure to liven up lunches and become a regular in your mealtime rotation.

Serves 4

Prep time
15 minutes

Pressure time
10 minutes

Release method
Natural

PREP INGREDIENTS

1 large potato, cubed

½ pound stew meat, cut into ½-inch cubes

1 onion, chopped

2 carrots, sliced

2 ribs celery, sliced

1 (8-ounce) can tomato sauce

Salt and pepper to taste

1 cup frozen peas

1 cup frozen green beans

SERVING DAY INGREDIENTS

3 cups chicken or vegetable stock

PREP DIRECTIONS

Bring a medium pot of salted water to a boil over high heat. Add the potato and blanch for 2 to 3 minutes. Drain and set aside in a single layer to cool. (A kitchen towel is useful for this task.) Combine the cooled potatoes with the stew meat, onion, carrots, celery, tomato sauce, and salt and pepper in a 1-gallon resealable freezer bag. Place the peas and green beans in a separate bag. Squeeze out the air, label, and place each bag in a round container to freeze into shape.

SERVING DAY DIRECTIONS

Add the stock and the contents of the larger package to the multi-cooker inner pot. Cook on high pressure for 10 minutes, and then let the pressure release naturally. Set the pot to Sauté. Add the peas and beans and cook for a few minutes until hot.

Serves 4

Prep time
15 minutes

Pressure time
5 minutes

Release method
Natural

Hearty Root Vegetable Soup

Hearty Root Vegetable Soup is a warming medley of potato, celery root, and parsnip. Garnish it like a souped-up (pun intended) baked potato with bacon, chives, shredded cheese, and sour cream!

PREP INGREDIENTS

1 large potato, peeled and cut into 2-inch cubes

1 small celery root, peeled and cut into 2-inch cubes

2 medium parsnips, peeled and diced

1 carrot, chopped

3 shallots, minced

1 rib celery, minced

3 cloves garlic, minced

3 tablespoons extra-virgin olive oil

Salt and pepper to taste

SERVING DAY INGREDIENTS

2 cups vegetable or chicken stock

PREP DIRECTIONS

Bring a large pot of salted water to a boil over high heat. Add the potato, celery root, and parsnips, and blanch for 2 minutes. Drain and set aside in a single layer to cool. (A kitchen towel is useful for this task.) Transfer the cooled vegetables to a 1-gallon resealable freezer bag along with the remaining prep ingredients. Squeeze out the air, label, and place in a round container to freeze into shape.

SERVING DAY DIRECTIONS

Add the stock and the contents of the package to the multi-cooker inner pot. Cook on high pressure for 5 minutes. Let the pressure release naturally. Use an immersion blender to puree the soup.

Cream of Pumpkin Soup

Win at fall cooking with this delicately spiced and creamy pumpkin soup. You can use another winter squash like butternut squash if you don't have pumpkin on hand.

Serves 4 to 6

Prep time
10 minutes

Pressure time
5 minutes

Release method
Natural (5 minutes)

PREP INGREDIENTS

2 pounds pumpkin or butternut squash, peeled, seeded, and cut into 1-inch cubes

1 onion, finely chopped

3 cloves garlic, minced

2 tablespoons chopped chives

½ teaspoon ground ginger (optional)

Pinch of nutmeg

Salt and pepper to taste

SERVING DAY INGREDIENTS

2 cups chicken or vegetable stock

1 cup heavy cream

PREP DIRECTIONS

Combine all the prep ingredients in a 1-gallon resealable freezer bag. Squeeze out the air, label, and place in a round container to freeze into shape.

SERVING DAY DIRECTIONS

Add the stock and the contents of the package to the multi-cooker inner pot. Cook on high pressure for 5 minutes. Let the pressure release naturally for 5 minutes, and then manually release any remaining pressure. Use an immersion blender to puree the soup and then stir in the heavy cream.

Vegetables

Fiesta Veggie Chili

Fiesta Veggie Chili couldn't be easier to throw together. A surprising ingredient, jarred salsa, does the heavy lifting and provides a ton of flavor in this vegetarian dish. Serve topped with shredded cheese and perhaps a dollop of sour cream.

Serves 4

Prep time
10 minutes

Pressure time
5 minutes

Release method
Natural (10 minutes)

PREP INGREDIENTS

2 (15.5-ounce) cans pinto or black beans, drained and rinsed

1 zucchini or yellow squash, halved lengthwise and cut into
½-inch-thick slices

1 tablespoon chili powder

1 (16-ounce) jar your favorite salsa

1 (6.7-ounce) jar sliced roasted red peppers, drained

2 tablespoons olive oil

Salt to taste

SERVING DAY INGREDIENTS

1 cup vegetable stock

PREP DIRECTIONS

Combine all the prep ingredients in a 1-gallon resealable freezer bag. Squeeze out the air, label, and place in a round container to freeze into shape.

SERVING DAY DIRECTIONS

Add the stock and the contents of the package to the multi-cooker inner pot. Cook on high pressure for 5 minutes. Let the pressure release naturally for 10 minutes, and then manually release any remaining pressure.

Serves 4 to 6

Prep time
5 minutes

Pressure time
4 minutes

Release method
Manual

Miso-Brown Sugar Carrots

If you're not familiar with miso, it's a delicious soybean paste that gives a savory flavor to everything it touches. Find it in the refrigerated section of your supermarket. It lasts almost forever in the refrigerator. Add it to soups, fish dishes, and these Miso-Brown Sugar Carrots.

PREP INGREDIENTS

1½ pounds carrots, peeled and cut into 2-inch slices

2 tablespoons white miso

1 tablespoon packed brown sugar

1 tablespoon canola oil

1 tablespoon soy sauce

SERVING DAY INGREDIENTS

1 cup vegetable stock

PREP DIRECTIONS

Combine all the prep ingredients in a 1-gallon resealable freezer bag. Squeeze out the air, label, and place in a round container to freeze into shape.

SERVING DAY DIRECTIONS

Add the stock and the contents of the package to the multi-cooker inner pot. Cook on high pressure for 4 minutes. Manually release the pressure.

Black Bean and Poblano Chili

Serves 4

Prep time
10 minutes

Pressure time
7 minutes

Release method
Natural (5 minutes)

Black Bean and Poblano Chili is vegetarian, but if you and your family eat meat, fresh chorizo would be a delicious addition here. Remove two links from the casings, cook them in a pan, breaking them up into chunks, and let the meat cool before adding it to your freezer ingredients. Can't find poblanos? Use cubanelle or regular red bell peppers instead.

PREP INGREDIENTS

2 (15.5-ounce) cans black beans, drained and rinsed

1 (14.5-ounce) can fire-roasted whole tomatoes, drained

2 tablespoons olive oil

1 onion, chopped

2 poblano peppers, seeded and chopped

3 cloves garlic, minced

1 (16-ounce) jar tomatillo salsa (salsa verde)

Salt and pepper to taste

SERVING DAY INGREDIENTS

1 cup vegetable stock

Chopped cilantro, for garnish (optional)

PREP DIRECTIONS

Combine all the prep ingredients in a 1-gallon resealable freezer bag. Squeeze out the air, label, and place in a round container to freeze into shape.

SERVING DAY DIRECTIONS

Add the stock and the contents of the package to the multi-cooker inner pot. Cook on high pressure for 7 minutes. Let the pressure release naturally for 5 minutes, and then manually release any remaining pressure. If desired, garnish with chopped cilantro.

Serves 4 to 6

Prep time
25 minutes

Pressure time
20 minutes

Release method
Natural

Spinach Lasagna

The key to a successful Spinach Lasagna is getting as much of the liquid out of the spinach as you possibly can to avoid a watery lasagna. Place a colander in a larger bowl and add the frozen spinach so that it drains as it thaws. Then press down on the spinach to squeeze out even more liquid. Transfer the drained spinach to paper towels and roll it between them.

PREP INGREDIENTS

1 (16-ounce) bag frozen chopped spinach, thawed (see headnote)

1 egg, lightly beaten

8 ounces shredded mozzarella cheese, divided

1 (15-ounce) container ricotta cheese

½ cup grated Parmesan cheese

Pinch ground nutmeg (optional)

¼ teaspoon salt

½ teaspoon black pepper

1 (25-ounce) jar tomato sauce (you may not need it all)

1 (9-ounce) package no-boil lasagna noodles (you may not need them all)

SERVING DAY INGREDIENTS

1½ cups water

PREP DIRECTIONS

In a medium bowl, stir together the drained spinach, egg, two-thirds of the mozzarella, the ricotta, Parmesan, a pinch of nutmeg, if using, and the salt and pepper. Spread a thin layer of sauce over the bottom of a 7-inch springform pan. Break up the uncooked lasagna noodles and place them in a single layer on the bottom of the pan. Spread a layer of the spinach-cheese mixture, then a layer of sauce. Top with another layer of noodles broken to fit. Continue layering, ending with a final layer of noodles and sauce. Top with the remaining one-third mozzarella cheese. Cover tightly with aluminum foil and freeze.

SERVING DAY DIRECTIONS

Thaw completely in the refrigerator. Add the water and the trivet to the bottom of the multi-cooker. Using a foil sling, gently lower the covered lasagna onto the trivet. Tuck in the foil ends and cook on high pressure for 20 minutes. Let the pressure release naturally for 10 minutes, and then manually release any remaining pressure. Check for doneness, adding more time if necessary. If desired, transfer the uncovered lasagna to the oven and broil for a few minutes until the cheese is golden brown. Let rest for 15 minutes before releasing from the springform pan and slicing.

Note: Unlike most of the other recipes in this book, the lasagna must be thawed in the refrigerator before cooking to avoid frozen spots.

Serves 4

Prep time
10 minutes

Pressure time
5 minutes

Release method
Natural (10 minutes)

Louisiana Red Beans

A no-fuss favorite in no time flat. All you need to do to whip up this Southern gem on any night of the week is to fire up the multi-cooker and cook a big pot of rice. If you're not vegetarian, feel free to add up to 8 ounces sliced andouille sausage to the prep ingredients, or serve it on the side on the day you prepare the dish.

PREP INGREDIENTS

2 (15.5-ounce) cans red kidney or small red beans, drained and rinsed

1 green bell pepper, seeded and chopped

1 onion, chopped

1 rib celery, chopped

4 cloves garlic, minced

2 tablespoons olive oil

1 tablespoon hot sauce (such as Tabasco)

1 teaspoon Cajun seasoning

Salt and pepper to taste

SERVING DAY INGREDIENTS

1 cup vegetable stock

Thinly sliced scallion, for garnish

PREP DIRECTIONS

Combine all the prep ingredients in a 1-gallon resealable freezer bag. Squeeze out the air, label, and place in a round container to freeze into shape.

SERVING DAY DIRECTIONS

Add the stock and the contents of the package to the multi-cooker inner pot. Cook on high pressure for 5 minutes. Let the pressure release naturally for 10 minutes, and then manually release any remaining pressure. Garnish with thinly sliced scallions. Pass more hot sauce at the table.

Sweet Potato Chili

Sweet and savory, this vegetarian chili is a delightful variation on your standard meat and beans chili. Plus, it's packed with good-for-you ingredients. Soy sauce might seem like an unusual addition, but it adds depth as well as seasoning.

Serves 4

Prep time
15 minutes

Pressure time
10 minutes

Release method
Natural (10 minutes)

PREP INGREDIENTS

1 sweet potato (about 1 pound), peeled and diced into ½-inch cubes

1 (15.5-ounce) can kidney beans or chickpeas, drained and rinsed

1 onion, chopped

3 cloves garlic, minced

1 (14.5-ounce) can diced tomatoes, drained

2 tablespoons chili powder

1 tablespoon soy sauce

½ teaspoon oregano

Salt and pepper to taste

SERVING DAY INGREDIENTS

1 cup vegetable stock

1 (8.5-ounce) can corn, drained

¼ cup chopped cilantro

PREP DIRECTIONS

Bring a medium pot of salted water to a boil over high heat. Add the sweet potato and blanch for 2 to 3 minutes. Drain and set aside in a single layer to cool. (A kitchen towel is useful for this task.) Add the cooled potatoes and the remaining prep ingredients to a 1-gallon resealable freezer bag. Squeeze out the air, label, and place in a round container to freeze into shape.

SERVING DAY DIRECTIONS

Add the stock and the contents of the package to the multi-cooker inner pot. Cook on high pressure for 10 minutes. Let the pressure release naturally for 10 minutes, and then manually release any remaining pressure. Stir in the corn and chopped cilantro.

Curried Chickpeas

Serves 4

Prep time
10 minutes

Pressure time
5 minutes

Release method
Natural (10 minutes)

Many Indian dishes require a long list of ingredients, but Curried Chickpeas, which is inspired by a traditional chana masala, uses just a handful of common spices that should be available in any supermarket. For maximum flavor, you can toast the spices in a dry pan until fragrant (don't let them burn), and then let them cool before adding them to your freezer bag.

PREP INGREDIENTS

2 (15.5-ounce) cans chickpeas, drained and rinsed

3 cloves garlic, chopped

1 tablespoon minced ginger

1 jalapeño or serrano chile, seeded and minced (optional)

1 tablespoon ground coriander

1 tablespoon ground cumin

1 teaspoon ground turmeric

2 tablespoons tomato paste

1 cup canned diced tomatoes

Salt and pepper to taste

SERVING DAY INGREDIENTS

1 cup vegetable stock

Juice of ½ lime or lemon

¼ cup chopped cilantro

PREP DIRECTIONS

Combine all the prep ingredients in a 1-gallon resealable freezer bag. Squeeze out the air, label, and place in a round container to freeze into shape.

SERVING DAY DIRECTIONS

Add the stock and the contents of the package to the multi-cooker inner pot. Cook on high pressure for 5 minutes. Let the pressure release naturally for 10 minutes, and then manually release any remaining pressure. Stir in the lime juice and chopped cilantro.

Serves 4

Prep time
10 minutes

Pressure time
12 minutes

Release method
Natural

Lentil Bolognese

Whether you're vegetarian, it's Meatless Monday, or you're looking for a leaner, lighter way to satisfy your pasta craving, don't knock Lentil Bolognese unless you've tried it. The soy sauce and optional dried mushrooms will up the savory, umami element, so you won't even miss the meat, and the red lentils break down beautifully into the sauce. Serve over pasta and garnish with torn basil leaves and grated Parmesan cheese.

PREP INGREDIENTS

1 cup dried red lentils, picked over for debris and rinsed

1 onion, finely chopped

1 carrot, peeled and chopped

2 cloves garlic, minced

Handful dried porcini mushrooms (optional)

2 tablespoons tomato paste

2 teaspoons soy sauce

1 (14.5-ounce) can crushed tomatoes

1 tablespoon Italian seasoning

Salt and pepper to taste

SERVING DAY INGREDIENTS

1 cup vegetable stock

PREP DIRECTIONS

Combine all the prep ingredients in a 1-gallon resealable freezer bag. Squeeze out the air, label, and place in a round container to freeze into shape.

SERVING DAY DIRECTIONS

Add the stock and the contents of the package to the multi-cooker inner pot. Cook on high pressure for 12 minutes. Let the pressure release naturally.

Soy-Ginger Carrots

It's 6 p.m. You've got your main course all set, but what's the veggie? Reach into the freezer and grab quick and easy Soy-Ginger Carrots. You can reduce the sauce at the end to make it more of a glaze and even stir in a teaspoon of sesame oil for a nutty flavor.

Serves 4 to 6

Prep time
10 minutes

Pressure time
4 minutes

Release method
Manual

PREP INGREDIENTS

1½ pounds carrots, peeled and cut into 2-inch pieces

1 tablespoon olive oil

1 tablespoon minced fresh ginger

1 tablespoon packed brown sugar

2 tablespoons soy sauce

1 teaspoon lime zest

SERVING DAY INGREDIENTS

1 cup vegetable stock

PREP DIRECTIONS

Combine all the prep ingredients in a 1-gallon resealable freezer bag. Squeeze out the air, label, and place in a round container to freeze into shape.

SERVING DAY DIRECTIONS

Add the stock and the contents of the package to the multi-cooker inner pot. Cook on high pressure for 4 minutes. Manually release the remaining pressure.

Serves 4

Prep time
10 minutes

Pressure time
4 minutes

Release method
Manual

Pumpkin Thai Red Curry

Thai flavors are like an explosion in the mouth: a little spicy, a little sweet, a little salty. Pumpkin Thai Red Curry is no exception. The pressure cooker makes the bell pepper quite soft, so if you prefer yours on the crisp side, don't add it to the prep bag. Just slice it up on serving day and add it at the end, simmering for a few minutes. If you're looking to add some vegetarian protein, stir in cubed tofu and let it heat through for 5 minutes or so in the finished curry. It will soak up lots of flavor. Serve over jasmine rice.

PREP INGREDIENTS

2 pounds pumpkin or butternut squash, peeled, seeded, and cut into bite-size pieces

1 green or red bell pepper, seeded and sliced

1 onion, thinly sliced

2 tablespoons packed brown sugar

2 tablespoons fish sauce (or soy sauce)

2 tablespoons red curry paste (or more to taste)

SERVING DAY INGREDIENTS

½ cup vegetable or chicken stock

1 cup coconut milk

½ cup thinly sliced basil leaves (Thai basil if possible)

PREP DIRECTIONS

Combine all the prep ingredients in a 1-gallon resealable freezer bag. Squeeze out the air, label, and place in a round container to freeze into shape.

SERVING DAY DIRECTIONS

Add the stock, coconut milk, and the contents of the package to the multi-cooker inner pot. Cook on high pressure for 4 minutes. Manually release the remaining pressure. Stir in the basil leaves.

Serves 4

Prep time
10 minutes

Pressure time
5 minutes

Release method
Natural

Mexican Tomato and Kidney Bean Stew

Bring some south-of-the-border flair into your week. This brightly flavored stew is delicious topped with avocado, fresh cilantro, and a squeeze of lime juice.

PREP INGREDIENTS

1 (28-ounce) can crushed fire-roasted tomatoes

1 (6.7-ounce) jar roasted red peppers, drained and sliced

1 (15.5-ounce) can dark kidney beans, drained and rinsed

3 tablespoons olive oil

1 cup frozen corn

1 jalapeño, chopped (seeded for less heat, if desired)

3 cloves garlic, minced

1 teaspoon ground cumin

1 teaspoon dried oregano

Salt and pepper to taste

SERVING DAY INGREDIENTS

2 cups vegetable stock

PREP DIRECTIONS

Combine all the prep ingredients in a 1-gallon resealable freezer bag. Squeeze out the air, label, and place in a round container to freeze into shape.

SERVING DAY DIRECTIONS

Add the stock and the contents of the package to the multi-cooker inner pot. Cook on high pressure for 5 minutes. Let the pressure release naturally.

Mediterranean Chickpeas with Sun-Dried Tomatoes and Artichokes

Serves 4

Prep time
10 minutes

Pressure time
5 minutes

Release method
Natural (10 minutes)

Oregano, rosemary, artichokes, olives, and sun-dried tomatoes—the flavors of the Mediterranean are bold and ready to wake you up out of your dinner slump! Serve Mediterranean Chickpeas with Sun-Dried Tomatoes and Artichokes with rice, orzo, or couscous.

PREP INGREDIENTS

2 (15.5-ounce) cans chickpeas, drained and rinsed

1 onion, chopped

1 plum tomato, chopped

3 cloves garlic, minced

¼ cup chopped sun-dried tomatoes in oil

1 teaspoon dried oregano

½ teaspoon dried rosemary

2 tablespoons olive oil

Salt and pepper to taste

SERVING DAY INGREDIENTS

1 cup vegetable stock

½ (9-ounce) package frozen artichokes

½ cup sliced black olives (optional)

¼ cup chopped fresh parsley (optional)

PREP DIRECTIONS

Combine all the prep ingredients in a 1-gallon resealable freezer bag. Squeeze out the air, label, and place in a round container to freeze into shape.

SERVING DAY DIRECTIONS

Add the stock and the contents of the package to the multi-cooker inner pot. Cook on high pressure for 5 minutes. Let the pressure release naturally for 10 minutes, and then manually release any remaining pressure. Set the pot to Sauté. Stir in the frozen artichokes and cook, stirring occasionally, until heated through. If desired, stir in the black olives and chopped fresh parsley.

Serves 4 to 6

Prep time
10 minutes

Pressure time
5 minutes

Release method
Natural (10 minutes)

Greek-Inspired Butter Beans

The gigande bean is a large white bean commonly used in Greek cuisine. It can be a little hard to find, so this recipe uses canned butter beans instead. You can serve Greek-Inspired Butter Beans as a side to a grilled meat dish or simply with rice and a salad for a delicious vegetarian meal.

PREP INGREDIENTS

2 (15.5-ounce) cans butter beans, drained and rinsed

½ onion, chopped

2 plum tomatoes, grated or diced

4 cloves garlic, minced

¼ cup chopped fresh parsley

¼ cup olive oil

1 tablespoon honey

Salt and pepper to taste

SERVING DAY INGREDIENTS

1 cup vegetable stock

Handful sliced almonds (optional)

Chopped fresh parsley (optional)

Lemon wedges, for garnish

PREP DIRECTIONS

Combine all the prep ingredients in a 1-gallon resealable freezer bag. Squeeze out the air, label, and place in a round container to freeze into shape.

SERVING DAY DIRECTIONS

Add the stock and the contents of the package to the multi-cooker inner pot. Cook on high pressure for 5 minutes. Let the pressure release naturally for 10 minutes, and then manually release any remaining pressure. Stir in the almonds and parsley, if using, and serve with lemon wedges.

Chicken & Turkey

Pulled Chicken Sliders

Much lighter than pork barbecue and just as tasty, Pulled Chicken Sliders are great simply with some shredded cabbage, but feel free to add coleslaw or even some provolone cheese. Because of the sugar content in the prep ingredients, this recipe uses a little bit more water to keep from scorching on the bottom of the pot. Just reduce the liquid to the consistency you're looking for at the end.

Serves 6 to 8
as sandwiches

Prep time
15 minutes

Pressure time
10 minutes

Release method
Natural (10 minutes)

PREP INGREDIENTS

2 pounds boneless, skinless chicken thighs, cut into 1½-inch chunks

1 small onion, chopped

3 cloves garlic, minced

1 cup ketchup

½ cup apple cider vinegar

½ cup packed brown sugar

2 tablespoons Worcestershire sauce

1 tablespoon hot sauce (such as Tabasco)

2 teaspoons dry mustard

SERVING DAY INGREDIENTS

1¼ cups chicken stock

PREP DIRECTIONS

Combine all the prep ingredients in a 1-gallon resealable freezer bag. Squeeze out the air, label, and place in a round container to freeze into shape.

SERVING DAY DIRECTIONS

Add the stock and the contents of the package to the multi-cooker inner pot. Cook on high pressure for 10 minutes. Let the pressure release naturally for 5 minutes, and then manually release any remaining pressure. Using a slotted spoon, transfer the chicken to a large bowl and shred it using two forks. Meanwhile, turn the pot to Sauté and reduce the liquid, stirring frequently, until it's like a glaze. Add some of the liquid to the chicken and toss to coat evenly. Serve on slider buns with shredded cabbage or coleslaw.

Serves 4 to 6

Prep time
15 minutes

Pressure time
10 minutes

Release method
Natural (10 minutes)

Chicken, Chorizo, and Chickpea Stew

For this dish, you want to make sure to pick up a Spanish-style chorizo, which is a cured sausage, instead of the fresh version. Your family will love this richly flavored stew that tastes like it cooked all day, and no one has to know it only took a few minutes to throw together.

PREP INGREDIENTS

1½ pounds boneless, skinless chicken thighs, sliced into ½-inch strips

½ pound dried Spanish chorizo, thinly sliced

1 (15.5-ounce) can chickpeas, drained and rinsed

1 onion, chopped

3 cloves garlic, minced

2 teaspoons paprika

1 teaspoon dried oregano

Salt and pepper to taste

SERVING DAY INGREDIENTS

1 cup chicken stock

Chopped parsley, for garnish (optional)

PREP DIRECTIONS

Combine all the prep ingredients in a 1-gallon resealable freezer bag. Squeeze out the air, label, and place in a round container to freeze into shape.

SERVING DAY DIRECTIONS

Add the stock and the contents of the package to the multi-cooker inner pot. Cook on high pressure for 10 minutes. Let the pressure release naturally for 10 minutes, and then manually release any remaining pressure. If desired, garnish with chopped parsley.

Kung Pao Chicken

Kung Pao Chicken is a Chinese restaurant favorite, and this version is a healthier alternative to takeout. If you want additional vegetables, feel free to throw a few handfuls of fresh or frozen veggies in at the end before adding the cornstarch mixture. Cook them for a few minutes just until they're crisp-tender.

Serves 4 to 6

Prep time
15 minutes

Pressure time
10 minutes

Release method
Natural (5 minutes)

PREP INGREDIENTS

2 pounds boneless, skinless chicken thighs, cut into 1½-inch chunks

1 red bell pepper, seeded and chopped

1 onion, chopped

3 cloves garlic, minced

1 tablespoon minced ginger

1 tablespoon white vinegar

2 tablespoons hoisin sauce

1 tablespoon Sriracha sauce

SERVING DAY INGREDIENTS

¾ cup chicken stock

¼ cup soy sauce

2 tablespoons cornstarch

3 tablespoons cold water

¼ cup coarsely chopped peanuts

2 sliced scallions, thinly

1 teaspoon sesame oil (optional)

PREP DIRECTIONS

Combine all the prep ingredients in a 1-gallon resealable freezer bag. Squeeze out the air, label, and place in a round container to freeze into shape.

SERVING DAY DIRECTIONS

Add the stock, soy sauce, and the contents of the package to the multi-cooker inner pot. Cook on high pressure for 10 minutes. Let the pressure release naturally for 5 minutes, and then manually release any remaining pressure. Meanwhile, in a small bowl, mix together the cornstarch and water. Set the pot to Sauté, and stir in the cornstarch mixture until the sauce is slightly thickened. Stir in the peanuts, scallions, and sesame oil (if using).

Serves 3 to 4

Prep time
10 minutes

Pressure time
10 minutes

Release method
Natural (10 minutes)

Mediterranean Chicken

The prep for this dish couldn't be simpler. Just cut up the chicken, measure a few herbs, and you're set. On serving day, you'll add a delicious mix of wine, olives, and parsley for an easy Mediterranean treat!

PREP INGREDIENTS

6 boneless, skinless chicken thighs, cut into 1½-inch pieces

1 cup canned diced tomatoes

2 tablespoons olive oil

3 cloves garlic, crushed

¼ teaspoon dried rosemary

½ teaspoon dried oregano

Salt to taste

SERVING DAY INGREDIENTS

½ cup dry white wine

½ cup chicken stock

¼ cup coarsely chopped oil-cured olives

2 tablespoons chopped parsley

PREP DIRECTIONS

Combine all the prep ingredients in a 1-gallon resealable freezer bag. Squeeze out the air, label, and place in a round container to freeze into shape.

SERVING DAY DIRECTIONS

Add the wine, stock, and the contents of the package to the multi-cooker inner pot. Cook on high pressure for 10 minutes. Let the pressure release naturally for 10 minutes, and then manually release any remaining pressure. Stir in the olives and chopped parsley.

Chicken Cacciatore

Chicken Cacciatore is a comforting, classic dish with countless variations. This one uses rich red wine for amazing depth of flavor. Italian seasoning, which is a mix of several herbs, keeps the prep simple. Serve with a side of pasta and top with grated Parmesan.

Serves 4

Prep time
15 minutes

Pressure time
10 minutes

Release method
Natural (5 minutes)

PREP INGREDIENTS

2 pounds boneless, skinless chicken thighs, cut into 1½-inch pieces

1 onion, chopped

3 cloves garlic, minced

1 (14.5-ounce) can diced tomatoes, drained

2 tablespoons tomato paste

1 tablespoon Italian seasoning

Salt to taste

SERVING DAY INGREDIENTS

½ cup dry red wine

½ cup chicken stock

PREP DIRECTIONS

Combine all the prep ingredients in a 1-gallon resealable freezer bag. Squeeze out the air, label, and place in a round container to freeze into shape.

SERVING DAY DIRECTIONS

Add the wine, chicken stock, and the contents of the package to the multi-cooker inner pot. Cook on high pressure for 10 minutes. Let the pressure release naturally for 5 minutes, and then manually release any remaining pressure.

Serves 4

Prep time
15 minutes

Pressure time
8 minutes

Release method
Natural (10 minutes)

Chicken Paprikash

One of the most famous Hungarian dishes, Chicken Paprikash uses a ton of delicious sweet paprika. It gives a wonderfully bright orange color and subtle flavor to the dish. Sour cream stirred in at the end adds creaminess. The key to this recipe is to use a Hungarian-style paprika; find it in a small tin in the spice aisle. Serve over buttered noodles.

PREP INGREDIENTS

2 pounds boneless, skinless chicken thighs, cut into 1½-inch chunks

1 onion, chopped

1 red bell pepper, seeded and sliced

1 plum tomato, seeded and chopped

2 tablespoons Hungarian sweet paprika

2 tablespoons tomato paste

Salt to taste

SERVING DAY INGREDIENTS

1 cup chicken stock

½ cup sour cream

PREP DIRECTIONS

Combine all the prep ingredients in a 1-gallon resealable freezer bag. Squeeze out the air, label, and place in a round container to freeze into shape.

SERVING DAY DIRECTIONS

Add the stock and the contents of the package to the multi-cooker inner pot. Cook on high pressure for 8 minutes. Let the pressure release naturally for 10 minutes, and then manually release any remaining pressure. If you wish, reduce the sauce to the desired consistency. Stir in the sour cream.

Serves 4 to 6

Prep time
15 minutes

Pressure time
8 minutes

Release method
Natural (10 minutes)

White Chicken Chili

Poblano peppers lend a mild spiciness and distinctive flavor to White Chicken Chili, but if you can't find them or don't like spice, use cubanelles (Italian frying peppers) or green bell peppers. Serve topped with shredded cheddar or Monterey Jack cheese and diced avocado.

PREP INGREDIENTS

1½ pounds boneless, skinless chicken thighs, cut into 1½-inch chunks

2 (15.5-ounce) cans white beans, such as cannellini or Great Northern, drained and rinsed

1 jalapeño pepper, seeded and diced (optional)

2 poblano peppers, seeded and chopped

1 onion, chopped

3 cloves garlic, minced

2 teaspoons ground cumin

1 teaspoon dried oregano

Salt and pepper to taste

SERVING DAY INGREDIENTS

1 cup chicken stock

2 to 3 tablespoons chopped cilantro or parsley

PREP DIRECTIONS

Combine all the prep ingredients in a 1-gallon resealable freezer bag. Squeeze out the air, label, and place in a round container to freeze into shape.

SERVING DAY DIRECTIONS

Add the stock and the contents of the package to the multi-cooker inner pot. Cook on high pressure for 8 minutes. Let the pressure release naturally for 10 minutes, and then manually release any remaining pressure. Stir in the cilantro.

Creamy Garlic-Lemon Chicken with Spinach

Serves 4

Prep time
10 minutes

Pressure time
8 minutes

Release method
Natural (10 minutes)

A pressure cooker tends to mellow the flavor of garlic, so to give Creamy Garlic-Lemon Chicken with Spinach a punch, stir in a teaspoon of raw minced garlic at the end. (You can always add more if you love garlic!) Serve this dish over egg noodles or penne.

PREP INGREDIENTS

2 pounds boneless, skinless chicken thighs, cut into 1½-inch chunks

5 cloves garlic, minced

Several sprigs fresh thyme or 1 teaspoon dried thyme

Zest of 1 lemon

1 tablespoon lemon juice

¼ cup white wine

Salt and pepper to taste

SERVING DAY INGREDIENTS

1 cup chicken stock

½ cup heavy cream

2 tablespoons unsalted butter

1 teaspoon minced garlic

1 (5-ounce) bag baby spinach

PREP DIRECTIONS

Combine all the prep ingredients in a 1-gallon resealable freezer bag. Squeeze out the air, label, and place in a round container to freeze into shape.

SERVING DAY DIRECTIONS

Add the stock and the contents of the package to the multi-cooker inner pot. Cook on high pressure for 8 minutes. Let the pressure release naturally for 10 minutes, and then manually release any remaining pressure. Remove the thyme sprigs. If the sauce is too thin, transfer the chicken to a plate and simmer until the sauce reaches the desired consistency. Stir in the heavy cream, butter, minced garlic, and baby spinach until the spinach is just wilted.

Sesame Orange Chicken

Sesame Orange Chicken is perfect for those nights when you're craving Chinese takeout. The secret ingredient? Orange marmalade! Serve over rice to soak up the delicious sauce.

Serves 4

Prep time
15 minutes

Pressure time
8 minutes

Release method
Natural (10 minutes)

PREP INGREDIENTS

1½ pounds boneless, skinless chicken thighs, cut into 1-inch pieces

3 cloves garlic, minced

1 tablespoon minced ginger

½ cup orange marmalade

¼ cup hoisin sauce

2 tablespoons soy sauce

1 tablespoon rice vinegar (or more as needed to balance sweetness)

SERVING DAY INGREDIENTS

1 cup chicken stock

2 tablespoons cornstarch

3 tablespoons cold water

2 scallions, thinly sliced

1 tablespoon sesame seeds

PREP DIRECTIONS

Combine all the prep ingredients in a 1-gallon resealable freezer bag. Squeeze out the air, label, and place in a round container to freeze into shape.

SERVING DAY DIRECTIONS

Add the stock and the contents of the package to the multi-cooker inner pot. Cook on high pressure for 8 minutes. Let the pressure release naturally for 10 minutes, and then release any remaining pressure. In a small bowl, stir together the cornstarch and water. Set the pot to Sauté, and stir in the cornstarch mixture until the sauce is slightly thickened. Stir in the scallions and sesame seeds.

Serves 4

Prep time
15 minutes

Pressure time
8 minutes

Release method
Natural (10 minutes)

Country Captain

A Southern favorite, Country Captain is packed with flavor—and has a great name to boot. Other variations exist, but what doesn't change is the mix of curry powder, raisins or currants, and almonds.

PREP INGREDIENTS

2 pounds boneless, skinless chicken thighs, cut into 2-inch chunks

1 medium onion, chopped

1 green bell pepper, seeded and chopped

1 cup canned diced tomatoes

1 tablespoon curry powder

½ teaspoon ground thyme

¼ cup raisins or currants

Salt and pepper to taste

SERVING DAY INGREDIENTS

1 cup chicken stock

¼ cup slivered or sliced almonds

PREP DIRECTIONS

Combine all the prep ingredients in a 1-gallon resealable freezer bag. Squeeze out the air, label, and place in a round container to freeze into shape.

COOKING DIRECTIONS

Add the stock and the contents of the package to the multi-cooker inner pot. Cook on high pressure for 8 minutes. Let the pressure release naturally for 10 minutes, and then manually release any remaining pressure. If the sauce is too thin, transfer the chicken to a plate and simmer until the sauce reaches the desired consistency. Garnish with the almonds.

Chicken in Red Wine Sauce

Serves 4

Prep time
15 minutes

Pressure time
8 minutes

Release method
Natural

Chicken in Red Wine Sauce is inspired by the French dish coq au vin, which uses a whole cut-up chicken. To simplify things for the multi-cooker, use boneless, skinless chicken thighs. If you wish, you can add 8 ounces sliced mushrooms before you thicken the sauce. Just cook them a few extra minutes until tender. Serve with crusty bread or mashed potatoes to soak up the sauce! *Bon appétit*!

PREP INGREDIENTS

2 pounds boneless, skinless chicken thighs, cut into 2-inch pieces

4 ounces pancetta or ham steak, diced

½ pound baby carrots, halved

1 onion, chopped

2 cloves garlic, minced

1 cup dry red wine

3 sprigs fresh thyme or ½ teaspoon dried thyme

1 bay leaf (optional)

Salt and pepper to taste

SERVING DAY INGREDIENTS

1 cup chicken stock

1 tablespoon cornstarch (optional)

2 tablespoons cold water (optional)

2 tablespoons unsalted butter

2 tablespoons chopped fresh parsley

PREP DIRECTIONS

Combine all the prep ingredients in a 1-gallon resealable freezer bag. Squeeze out the air, label, and place in a round container to freeze into shape.

SERVING DAY DIRECTIONS

Add the stock and the contents of the package to the multi-cooker inner pot. Cook on high pressure for 8 minutes. Let the pressure release naturally. If the sauce is too thin, in a small bowl, stir together the cornstarch and water. Set the pot to Sauté, and stir in the cornstarch mixture until the sauce is slightly thickened. Stir in the butter and fresh parsley. Remove the bay leaf and thyme sprigs before serving.

Serves 4

Prep time
5 minutes

Pressure time
15 minutes

Release method
Natural (10 minutes)

Sweet and Tangy Honey-Mustard Chicken

No chopping is needed to prep Sweet and Tangy Honey-Mustard Chicken! To get a beautifully bronzed and crispy skin, stick the drumsticks under the broiler for a few minutes.

PREP INGREDIENTS

⅓ cup whole-grain mustard

½ cup honey

2 tablespoons apple cider vinegar

1 tablespoon soy sauce

½ teaspoon salt

¼ teaspoon pepper

2 pounds chicken drumsticks

SERVING DAY INGREDIENTS

1 cup chicken stock

PREP DIRECTIONS

In a small freezer container, stir together the mustard, honey, vinegar, soy sauce, salt, and pepper. Seal tightly and freeze. In a large resealable freezer bag, add the chicken drumsticks. Place them on a large freezer-safe pan so that they lie flat and freeze individually. You may need to use more than one bag.

SERVING DAY DIRECTIONS

Add the stock, the chicken, and the contents of the sauce container to the multi-cooker inner pot. Cook on high pressure for 15 minutes. Let the pressure release naturally for 10 minutes, and then manually release any remaining pressure. Transfer the chicken to a serving dish. If desired, crisp up the skin for a few minutes under the broiler. Meanwhile, reduce the sauce, stirring occasionally, until it's the consistency of a glaze. Spoon the glaze over the chicken.

Serves 4

Prep time
15 minutes

Pressure time
8 minutes

Release method
Natural (10 minutes)

Fennel and Lemon Chicken

Fennel, which can be eaten raw or cooked, has a mild anise flavor that goes well with lemon and chicken. It's a nice variation on the weeknight chicken dinner routine.

PREP INGREDIENTS

2 pounds boneless, skinless chicken thighs, cut into 1½-inch chunks

1 large bulb fennel, thinly sliced

3 cloves garlic, minced

1 tablespoon lemon juice

Salt and pepper to taste

SERVING DAY INGREDIENTS

1 cup chicken stock

1 tablespoon cornstarch (optional)

2 tablespoons cold water (optional)

2 tablespoons unsalted butter

Lemon wedges, for serving

PREP DIRECTIONS

Combine all the prep ingredients in a 1-gallon resealable freezer bag. Squeeze out the air, label, and place in a round container to freeze into shape.

SERVING DAY DIRECTIONS

Add the stock and the contents of the package to the multi-cooker inner pot. Cook on high pressure for 8 minutes. Let the pressure release naturally for 10 minutes, and then manually release any remaining pressure. If the sauce is too thin, in a small bowl, stir together the cornstarch and water. Set the pot to Sauté, and stir in the cornstarch mixture until the sauce is slightly thickened. Stir in the butter until melted. Serve with lemon wedges.

Chicken Tinga

Liven up Taco Tuesday with Chicken Tinga, a delicious dish of shredded chicken in a roasted tomato–chipotle sauce. Serve on corn tortillas with sliced avocado and crumbled Mexican cheese, such as cotija.

Serves 4 to 6

Prep time
15 minutes

Pressure time
8 minutes

Release method
Natural (10 minutes)

PREP INGREDIENTS

2 pounds boneless, skinless chicken thighs, cut into 1-inch chunks

1 onion, chopped

3 cloves garlic, minced

½ cup jarred tomatillo salsa

½ (15-ounce) can fire-roasted tomatoes

1 tablespoon minced canned chipotle pepper in adobo

1 tablespoon Worcestershire sauce

1 teaspoon dried oregano

Salt and pepper to taste

SERVING DAY INGREDIENTS

1 cup chicken stock

PREP DIRECTIONS

Combine all the prep ingredients in a 1-gallon resealable freezer bag. Squeeze out the air, label, and place in a round container to freeze into shape.

SERVING DAY DIRECTIONS

Add the stock and the contents of the package to the multi-cooker inner pot. Cook on high pressure for 8 minutes. Let the pressure release naturally for 10 minutes, and then manually release any remaining pressure.

Serves 4

Prep time
10 minutes

Pressure time
8 minutes

Release method
Natural (10 minutes)

Creamy Sun-Dried Tomato Chicken

Delicious over bow-tie pasta, Creamy Sun-Dried Tomato Chicken is so simple and so good. Serve over pasta with additional Parmesan cheese and a nice big green salad.

PREP INGREDIENTS

2 pounds boneless, skinless chicken thighs

½ cup chopped sun-dried tomatoes in oil

2 cloves garlic, minced

1 tablespoon red wine vinegar

2 teaspoons Italian seasoning

Salt to taste

SERVING DAY INGREDIENTS

1 cup chicken stock

½ cup grated Parmesan cheese

½ cup heavy cream

½ cup thinly sliced basil leaves

PREP DIRECTIONS

Combine all the prep ingredients in a 1-gallon resealable freezer bag. Squeeze out the air, label, and place in a round container to freeze into shape.

SERVING DAY DIRECTIONS

Add the stock and the contents of the package to the multi-cooker inner pot. Cook on high pressure for 8 minutes. Let the pressure release naturally for 10 minutes, and then manually release any remaining pressure. Stir in the Parmesan, heavy cream, and basil leaves.

Bourbon Chicken

A popular Cajun-Chinese dish, Bourbon Chicken was supposedly named after Bourbon Street in New Orleans. It's sweet and savory and will leave you craving more. It's also made with ingredients you probably already have on hand, so you can get cooking right away. Serve over rice with sliced scallions.

Serves 4

Prep time
15 minutes

Pressure time
8 minutes

Release method
Natural (10 minutes)

PREP INGREDIENTS

2 pounds boneless, skinless chicken thighs, cut into 1-inch chunks

½ onion, chopped

2 teaspoons minced fresh ginger

3 cloves garlic, minced

Pinch of crushed red pepper flakes (optional)

½ cup soy sauce

½ cup packed light or dark brown sugar

2 tablespoons ketchup

1 tablespoon rice vinegar

SERVING DAY INGREDIENTS

¼ cup apple juice

¾ cup chicken stock

2 tablespoons cornstarch

3 tablespoons cold water

PREP DIRECTIONS

Combine all the prep ingredients in a 1-gallon resealable freezer bag. Squeeze out the air, label, and place in a round container to freeze into shape.

SERVING DAY DIRECTIONS

Add the apple juice, the chicken stock and the contents of the package to the multi-cooker inner pot. Cook on high pressure for 8 minutes. Let the pressure release naturally for 10 minutes, and then release any remaining pressure. In a small bowl, stir together the cornstarch and water. Set the pot to Sauté, and stir in the cornstarch mixture until the sauce is slightly thickened.

Classic Buffalo Wings

For that game-day party, it can be a lifesaver to have at least one dish you can prepare in the multi-cooker, and for this recipe, you don't even need to prep anything. Just keep a bag of frozen wings in the freezer! If you prefer to freeze fresh wings, cut each whole wing into two pieces, discarding the wing tip. To prevent the wings from freezing into a giant block, place the wings on a lined baking sheet and freeze. Once they are frozen, you can transfer them a resealable freezer bag. Serve with blue cheese and celery.

Serves 4 to 6

Pressure time
8 minutes

Release method
Natural (10 minutes)

PREP INGREDIENTS

24 frozen chicken wings (see headnote)

SERVING DAY INGREDIENTS

1 cup water

6 tablespoons unsalted butter, melted

⅓ cup hot sauce (such as Frank's)

1 clove garlic, minced

SERVING DAY DIRECTIONS

Add the water and the trivet to the inner pot. Place the wings on top of the trivet. Cook on high pressure for 8 minutes. Let the pressure release naturally for 10 minutes, and then manually release any remaining pressure. Meanwhile, in a large bowl, stir together the melted butter, hot sauce, and minced garlic. Set the oven to broil. Transfer the wings to a nonstick baking sheet and brush lightly with the sauce. Transfer the baking sheet to the broiler and broil until light golden brown and crispy. Flip, brush the other side with the buffalo sauce, and return to the broiler. Carefully transfer the crispy wings to the bowl and toss with the remaining sauce.

Serves 4 to 6

Pressure time
8 minutes

Release method
Natural (10 minutes)

Honey-Mustard Wings

For Honey-Mustard Wings, you can use either spicy brown or Dijon mustard, whichever you prefer. Mix up the sauce while the wings are in the multi-cooker, put the wings under the broiler, toss to coat, and *voilà*—delicious wings any night of the week!

PREP INGREDIENTS

24 frozen chicken wings
(see headnote, page 81)

SERVING DAY INGREDIENTS

1 cup water

4 tablespoons unsalted butter, melted

⅓ cup spicy brown or Dijon mustard

¼ cup honey

1 clove garlic, minced

PREP DIRECTIONS

Add the water and the trivet to the inner pot. Place the wings on top of the trivet. Cook on high pressure for 8 minutes. Let the pressure release naturally for 10 minutes, and then manually release any remaining pressure. Meanwhile, in a large bowl, stir together the melted butter, mustard, honey, and garlic. You can add more mustard or honey to taste. Set the oven to broil. Transfer the wings to a nonstick baking sheet and brush lightly with the sauce. Transfer the baking sheet to the broiler and broil until light golden brown and crispy. Flip, brush the other side with the sauce, and return to the broiler. Carefully transfer the crispy wings to the bowl and toss with the remaining sauce.

Rosemary-Balsamic Chicken

Serves 4

Prep time
15 minutes

Pressure time
8 minutes

Release method
Natural

Rosemary and balsamic vinegar are great partners whose flavors complement each other perfectly, and this chicken dish couldn't be easier to throw together. It's ideal served with some tasty oven-roasted potatoes.

PREP INGREDIENTS

2 pounds boneless, skinless chicken thighs, cut into 2-inch chunks

2 tablespoons balsamic vinegar

2 tablespoons olive oil

2 teaspoons chopped fresh rosemary

3 cloves garlic, minced

Zest of 1 lemon

Salt and pepper to taste

SERVING DAY INGREDIENTS

1 cup chicken stock

Lemon wedges, for serving

PREP DIRECTIONS

Combine all the prep ingredients in a 1-gallon resealable freezer bag. Squeeze out the air, label, and place in a round container to freeze into shape.

SERVING DAY DIRECTIONS

Add the stock and the contents of the package to the multi-cooker inner pot. Cook on high pressure for 8 minutes. Let the pressure release naturally. Serve with lemon wedges.

Serves 4

Prep time
15 minutes

Pressure time
8 minutes

Release method
Natural (10 minutes)

Sweet and Sour Chicken

With pineapple chunks and bell pepper, Sweet and Sour Chicken is an all-time favorite. Now you don't even have to leave the house to get it when the craving strikes. Just reach in the freezer and pop it in the multi-cooker! For a contrast in textures, add some fresh veggies like snow peas at the end and let them cook for a minute or two. You can even garnish it with chunks of fresh pineapple. Serve over rice.

PREP INGREDIENTS

1½ pounds boneless, skinless chicken thighs, cut into 1-inch chunks

2 bell peppers, seeded and cut into 1-inch chunks

1 onion, cut into 1-inch chunks

1 (10-ounce) can pineapple chunks, drained

1 teaspoon ground ginger

3 tablespoons white or apple cider vinegar

2 tablespoons soy sauce

1 tablespoon canola oil

¼ cup packed brown sugar

3 tablespoons ketchup

Salt to taste

SERVING DAY INGREDIENTS

1 cup chicken stock

2 tablespoons cornstarch

3 tablespoons cold water

1 cup snow peas (optional)

PREP DIRECTIONS

Combine all the prep ingredients in a 1-gallon resealable freezer bag. Squeeze out the air, label, and place in a round container to freeze into shape.

SERVING DAY DIRECTIONS

Add the stock and the contents of the package to the multi-cooker inner pot. Cook on high pressure for 8 minutes. Let the pressure release naturally for 10 minutes, and then manually release any remaining pressure. In a small bowl, stir together the cornstarch and water. Set the pot to Sauté, and stir in the cornstarch mixture until the sauce is slightly thickened. If desired, when you add the cornstarch, you can also stir in the snow peas.

Ginger Chicken with Broccoli

Serves 4

Prep time
10 minutes

Pressure time
8 minutes

Release method
Natural (10 minutes)

Served with rice, Ginger Chicken with Broccoli is a complete meal! To keep the broccoli from disintegrating in the pressure-cooking process, it's added at the end and cooked for just a few minutes. You can buy a bag of frozen broccoli and keep it in the freezer next to your ginger chicken, or cut some up fresh on serving day. Cook it to your desired tenderness.

PREP INGREDIENTS

1 pound boneless, skinless chicken thighs, cut into 1-inch pieces

1 tablespoon minced fresh ginger

3 cloves garlic, minced

2 tablespoons canola oil

¼ cup packed brown sugar

1 tablespoon oyster sauce

2 tablespoons soy sauce

SERVING DAY INGREDIENTS

1 cup chicken stock

1 (16-ounce) package frozen broccoli

2 tablespoons cornstarch

3 tablespoons cold water

1 tablespoon sesame seeds (optional)

PREP DIRECTIONS

Combine all the prep ingredients in a 1-gallon resealable freezer bag. Squeeze out the air, label, and place in a round container to freeze into shape.

SERVING DAY DIRECTIONS

Add the stock and the contents of the package to the multi-cooker inner pot. Cook on high pressure for 8 minutes. Let the pressure release naturally for 10 minutes, and then manually release any remaining pressure. Set the pot on Sauté. Stir in the frozen broccoli and cook until heated through. In a small bowl, mix together the cornstarch and water. Stir in the cornstarch mixture and cook until the sauce is thickened. If desired, sprinkle with the sesame seeds.

Serves 4

Prep time
15 minutes

Pressure time
8 minutes

Release method
Natural

Cashew Chicken

How does tender chicken in a delicious sauce of garlic, soy sauce, and oyster sauce with crunchy cashews sound? Sounds great, and it's even better when it's waiting for you in the freezer! It's not essential to toast the cashews, but it's definitely worth it for the delicious roasted flavor. Garnish with sliced scallions and serve over rice.

PREP INGREDIENTS

1½ pounds boneless, skinless chicken thighs, cut into 1-inch chunks

1 carrot, peeled and thinly sliced

1 rib celery, thinly sliced

1 green or red bell pepper, seeded and cut into 1-inch chunks

1 tablespoon minced ginger

3 cloves garlic, minced

2 tablespoons soy sauce

2 tablespoons dry sherry

1 tablespoon oyster sauce

Salt to taste

SERVING DAY INGREDIENTS

1 cup chicken stock

⅓ cup cashews

2 cups frozen broccoli, thawed

2 tablespoons cornstarch

3 tablespoons cold water

PREP DIRECTIONS

Combine all the prep ingredients in a 1-gallon resealable freezer bag. Squeeze out the air, label, and place in a round container to freeze into shape.

SERVING DAY DIRECTIONS

Add the stock and the contents of the package to the multi-cooker inner pot. Cook on high pressure for 8 minutes. Let the pressure release naturally for 10 minutes, and then manually release any remaining pressure. Meanwhile, place the cashews in a dry skillet over medium heat. Toast, stirring occasionally, until lightly browned, 3 to 4 minutes. Set aside. Add the broccoli to the pot and stir to combine. In a small bowl, stir together the cornstarch and water. Set the pot to Sauté, and stir in the reserved cashews and the cornstarch mixture. Cook, stirring, until the sauce is slightly thickened and the broccoli is heated through.

Turkey and Bean Burritos

Serves 4

Prep time
10 minutes

Pressure time
5 minutes

Release method
Natural (5 minutes)

Turkey and Bean Burritos are all about maximum flavor for minimum effort, perfect for those hectic nights when the thought of cooking anything is enough to send you to the kitchen . . . in search of your stash of takeout menus. All you need are some flour tortillas, a few toppings, and a few minutes, and dinner is solved.

PREP INGREDIENTS

1 tablespoon olive oil

1 pound ground turkey

1 (1-ounce) package taco seasoning mix

1 (15.5-ounce) can black, pinto, or kidney beans, rinsed and drained

1 cup your favorite jarred salsa

¼ cup chopped fresh cilantro

SERVING DAY INGREDIENTS

1 cup chicken stock

PREP DIRECTIONS

Heat the olive oil in a medium nonstick skillet over medium heat. Add the turkey and cook, breaking up large chunks with a wooden spoon, until browned. Drain the excess fat, if any. Add the taco seasoning and water, according to package instructions. Cook until the mixture is slightly reduced and thickened, 3 to 5 minutes. Set aside to cool. Add the turkey, along the with the remaining prep ingredients, to a 1-gallon resealable freezer bag. Squeeze out the air, label, and place in a round container to freeze into shape.

SERVING DAY DIRECTIONS

Add the stock and the contents of the package to the multi-cooker inner pot. Cook on high pressure for 5 minutes. Let the pressure release naturally for 5 minutes, and then release any remaining pressure. Portion into flour tortillas, add toppings like cheese, avocado, lettuce, and sour cream, and roll up.

Serves 4

Prep time
15 minutes

Pressure time
8 minutes

Release method
Natural (10 minutes)

Chicken and Sausage Stew

Chicken *and* sausage? Why not! The flavor from the sausage permeates the stew, and the peppers, wine, and vinegar add layers of deliciousness. Serve over polenta or with pasta.

PREP INGREDIENTS

1 pound boneless, skinless chicken thighs, cut into 1-inch chunks

1 pound Italian sausage, cut into 1-inch slices

2 bell peppers, seeded and sliced

1 onion, chopped

3 cloves garlic, minced

2 tablespoons balsamic vinegar

¼ cup dry red wine

Salt to taste

SERVING DAY INGREDIENTS

1 cup chicken stock

Sliced basil leaves, for garnish (optional)

PREP DIRECTIONS

Combine all the prep ingredients in a 1-gallon resealable freezer bag. Squeeze out the air, label, and place in a round container to freeze into shape.

SERVING DAY DIRECTIONS

Add the stock and the contents of the package to the multi-cooker inner pot. Cook on high pressure for 8 minutes. Let the pressure release naturally for 10 minutes, and then manually release any remaining pressure. Garnish with sliced basil, if desired.

Potsticker Meatballs

If you love dumplings or potstickers, you'll love Potsticker Meatballs, which taste just like them—without the wrappers, of course. Don't forget the dipping sauce!

Serves 4

Prep time
20 minutes

Pressure time
7 minutes

Release method
Natural (5 minutes)

PREP INGREDIENTS

1½ pounds ground turkey or pork

2 cloves garlic, minced

2 teaspoons minced fresh ginger

3 tablespoons soy sauce

1 tablespoon toasted sesame oil

1 tablespoon dry sherry

1 tablespoon hoisin or oyster sauce

¼ cup panko breadcrumbs

¼ cup chopped fresh cilantro (optional)

3 scallions, minced

¼ teaspoon salt

½ teaspoon white pepper

SERVING DAY INGREDIENTS

1½ cups plus 2 tablespoons water, divided

½ cup soy sauce

2 tablespoons rice vinegar

1 teaspoon toasted sesame oil

PREP DIRECTIONS

In a large bowl, mix together all of the prep ingredients. Roll the mixture into 1½-inch balls, place on a parchment paper-lined baking sheet, and freeze. Once the meatballs are completely frozen, transfer them to a 1-gallon resealable freezer bag. Squeeze out the air, label, and place in a round container to freeze into shape.

SERVING DAY DIRECTIONS

Add 1½ cups of the water and the trivet to the multi-cooker inner pot. Place a steamer basket on top of the trivet and add the meatballs. Cook on high pressure for 7 minutes. Let the pressure release naturally for 10 minutes, and then manually release any remaining pressure. For the dipping sauce, mix together the soy sauce, vinegar, sesame oil, and remaining 2 tablespoons water in a small bowl, or use your favorite prepared version.

Serves 4 to 6

Prep time
15 minutes

Pressure time
8 minutes

Release method
Natural (10 minutes)

Cajun-Spiced Turkey and Black-Eyed Peas

Think of Cajun-Spiced Turkey and Black-Eyed Peas like a sort of southern chili! Cajun seasoning is a mix of paprika, cayenne, garlic powder, and other herbs and spices and is usually available in the spice aisle. It can be used with all kinds of foods, like fish, gumbo, jambalaya, potatoes, and meats.

PREP INGREDIENTS

1 pound ground turkey, browned and cooled

2 (15.5-ounce) cans black-eyed peas, drained and rinsed

4 cloves garlic, minced

1 tablespoon Cajun seasoning

1 jalapeño pepper, thinly sliced (seeded for less heat, if desired)

2 tablespoons tomato paste

Salt to taste

SERVING DAY INGREDIENTS

1 cup chicken stock

PREP DIRECTIONS

Combine all the prep ingredients in a 1-gallon resealable freezer bag. Squeeze out the air, label, and place in a round container to freeze into shape.

SERVING DAY DIRECTIONS

Add the stock and the contents of the package to the multi-cooker inner pot. Cook on high pressure for 8 minutes. Let the pressure release naturally for 10 minutes, and then manually release any remaining pressure.

Serves 4 to 6

Prep time
10 minutes

Pressure time
8 minutes

Release method
Natural (10 minutes)

Beer-Braised Turkey Tacos

Super simple and packed with flavor, Beer-Braised Turkey Tacos are great on either hard or soft shell tacos with a little cheese, sour cream, diced tomato, and corn. Use whatever kind of beer you have on hand!

PREP INGREDIENTS

2 pounds boneless, skinless turkey breast, cut into 2-inch chunks

1 jalapeño pepper, chopped, seeded if desired (optional)

1 (8-ounce) can tomato sauce

1 (4.5-ounce) can green chiles

1 tablespoon Worcestershire sauce

2 tablespoons chili powder

Salt and pepper to taste

SERVING DAY INGREDIENTS

½ cup beer

½ cup chicken stock

PREP DIRECTIONS

Combine all the prep ingredients in a 1-gallon resealable freezer bag. Squeeze out the air, label, and place in a round container to freeze into shape.

SERVING DAY DIRECTIONS

Add the beer, the chicken stock, and the contents of the package to the multi-cooker inner pot. Cook on high pressure for 8 minutes. Let the pressure release naturally for 10 minutes, and then manually release any remaining pressure. Shred softened turkey with two forks.

Beef & Pork

Serves 4 to 6

Prep time
15 minutes

Pressure time
20 minutes

Release method
Natural

Classic Pot Roast

Everyone needs a tasty basic pot roast recipe in their back pocket, and here's yours. By cutting the meat into chunks, you speed the cooking process and ensure the roast isn't still frozen solid when you've got a table full of hungry kids clamoring for dinner. Serve with roasted or baked potatoes, of course!

PREP INGREDIENTS

2 pounds chuck roast, cut into 2-inch chunks

2 large onions, cut into wedges

2 carrots, peeled and sliced into 2-inch pieces

2 ribs celery, cut into 2-inch pieces

1 bay leaf

2 teaspoons salt

1 teaspoon black pepper

2 sprigs fresh rosemary

2 sprigs fresh thyme

SERVING DAY INGREDIENTS

½ cup dry red wine

½ cup chicken stock

2 tablespoons cornstarch

3 tablespoons cold water

PREP DIRECTIONS

Combine all the prep ingredients in a 1-gallon resealable freezer bag. Squeeze out the air, label, and place in a round container to freeze into shape.

SERVING DAY DIRECTIONS

Add the red wine and the chicken stock (or use all chicken stock) and the contents of the package to the multi-cooker inner pot. Cook on high pressure for 20 minutes, and then let the pressure release naturally. Remove and discard the bay leaf and herb sprigs. Remove the meat and vegetables to a serving dish and tent with foil. Set the pot on Sauté and reduce the sauce to the desired consistency. In a small bowl, mix together the cornstarch and water. Set the pot to Sauté, and stir in the cornstarch mixture until the sauce is slightly thickened. Spoon the sauce over the meat and vegetables.

Serves 4

Prep time
15 minutes

Pressure time
7 minutes

Release method
Natural

Easy Beef and Bean Chili

Everyone needs an easy, tasty chili that you can get on the table quickly. This one has a smoky and spicy twist with the addition of chipotle peppers, but you can leave them out if you don't happen to have a can on hand; you can also substitute a teaspoon of smoked paprika. Add your favorite chili toppings, such as cheese, sour cream, crushed corn chips, diced avocado, chopped onion, and cilantro.

PREP INGREDIENTS

1 pound ground beef, browned and cooled

1 (15.5-ounce) can kidney or pinto beans, drained and rinsed

1 (14.5-ounce) can diced tomatoes, drained

1 bell pepper, seeded and thinly sliced

1 onion, chopped

2 cloves garlic, minced

2 tablespoons chili powder

1 teaspoon ground cumin

1 teaspoon dried oregano

2 teaspoons chopped canned chipotle pepper in adobo

Salt to taste

SERVING DAY INGREDIENTS

1 cup chicken or beef stock

PREP DIRECTIONS

Combine all the prep ingredients in a 1-gallon resealable freezer bag. Squeeze out the air, label, and place in a round container to freeze into shape.

SERVING DAY DIRECTIONS

Add the stock and the contents of the package to the multi-cooker inner pot. Cook on high pressure for 7 minutes. Let the pressure release naturally for 5 minutes, and then manually release any remaining pressure.

Italian Pot Roast

This Italian Pot Roast combines tender chunks of beef, fragrant herbs, tomatoes, wine, and even tangy pepperoncini! It's delicious over polenta.

Serves 4 to 6

Prep time
15 minutes

Pressure time
20 minutes

Release method
Natural

PREP INGREDIENTS

2 pounds chuck roast, cut into 2-inch cubes

1 onion, chopped

3 cloves garlic, minced

1 carrot, peeled and chopped

1 rib celery, chopped

4 jarred pepperoncini, sliced (optional)

1 tablespoon Italian seasoning

2 tablespoons tomato paste

1 (14.5-ounce) can crushed tomatoes

Salt and pepper to taste

SERVING DAY INGREDIENTS

½ cup dry red wine

½ cup chicken stock

PREP DIRECTIONS

Combine all the prep ingredients in a 1-gallon resealable freezer bag. Squeeze out the air, label, and place in a round container to freeze into shape.

SERVING DAY DIRECTIONS

Add the wine, stock, and the contents of the package to the multi-cooker inner pot. Cook on high pressure for 20 minutes, and then let the pressure release naturally.

Beef Goulash

Goulash can refer to many different dishes from many different countries, but it originated in Hungary. Just as with Chicken Paprikash, you want to use a Hungarian-style paprika for the best flavor. Serve over buttered noodles or rice with dollops of sour cream. For another variation, substitute the chuck roast with boneless pork shoulder.

Serves 4

Prep time
10 minutes

Pressure time
20 minutes

Release method
Natural

PREP INGREDIENTS

2 pounds chuck roast, cut into 1-inch cubes

2 onions, coarsely chopped

2 green bell peppers, seeded and chopped

Salt and pepper to taste

2 tablespoons Hungarian sweet paprika

SERVING DAY INGREDIENTS

1 cup beef stock

2 tablespoons unsalted butter

PREP DIRECTIONS

Combine all the prep ingredients in a 1-gallon resealable freezer bag. Squeeze out the air, label, and place in a round container to freeze into shape.

SERVING DAY DIRECTIONS

Add the beef stock and the contents of the package to the multi-cooker inner pot. Cook on high pressure for 20 minutes, and then let the pressure release naturally. Stir in the butter until melted.

Serves 6 to 8

Prep time
15 minutes

Pressure time
20 minutes

Release method
Natural

Guinness Stew

Guinness Stew takes advantage of the rich flavors of Ireland's top brew. While this beef stew normally takes hours to make, you can have it any night of the week. You'll relax knowing it's waiting for you at home in the freezer whenever the craving strikes. You can also substitute lamb for the beef. Serve with mashed potatoes—and Guinness.

PREP INGREDIENTS

2 pounds chuck roast, cut into 1-inch chunks

1 onion, chopped

2 carrots, peeled and cut into 2-inch pieces

1 rib celery, chopped

1 tablespoon Worcestershire sauce

2 tablespoons dehydrated onion flakes (optional)

2 tablespoons tomato paste

1 beef bouillon cube

1 sprig fresh rosemary or ¼ teaspoon dried rosemary

3 or 4 sprigs fresh thyme or ½ teaspoon dried thyme

Salt and pepper to taste

SERVING DAY INGREDIENTS

1 cup Guinness

1 pound potatoes, peeled and cubed

2 tablespoons unsalted butter, softened

2 tablespoons all-purpose flour

Chopped fresh parsley, for garnish (optional)

PREP DIRECTIONS

Combine all the prep ingredients in a 1-gallon resealable freezer bag. Squeeze out the air, label, and place in a round container to freeze into shape.

SERVING DAY DIRECTIONS

Add the Guinness and the contents of the package to the multi-cooker inner pot. Cook on high pressure for 20 minutes, and then let the pressure release naturally. Meanwhile, place the potatoes a large pot of salted water. Bring to a boil, lower the heat, and simmer until just tender. Drain. Stir the potatoes into the stew. To thicken the stew, in a small bowl, mash together the butter and flour. Set the pot to Sauté and stir in the butter mixture until the sauce is thickened to the desired consistency. If you used fresh rosemary and thyme springs, remove and discard. If desired, sprinkle your stew with chopped fresh parsley before serving.

No-Bean Bowl of Red

A Texas-style chili doesn't include beans and is often known as "bowl of red." This freezer version builds flavor with smoky chipotle and beef stock. When it's done, the beef should fall apart when pierced with a fork.

Serves 4

Prep time
15 minutes

Pressure time
20 minutes

Release method
Natural

PREP INGREDIENTS

2 pounds chuck roast, cut into 1-inch cubes

1 tablespoon minced canned chipotle pepper in adobo

1 onion, chopped

3 cloves garlic, chopped

1 jalapeño pepper, chopped, seeded if desired (optional)

2 tablespoons chili powder

1 teaspoon dried oregano

1 teaspoon ground cumin

1 tablespoon packed brown sugar

1 teaspoon salt

1 (14.5-ounce) can crushed tomatoes

SERVING DAY INGREDIENTS

1 cup chicken or beef stock

PREP DIRECTIONS

Combine all the prep ingredients in a 1-gallon resealable freezer bag. Squeeze out the air, label, and place in a round container to freeze into shape.

SERVING DAY DIRECTIONS

Add the stock and the contents of the package to the multi-cooker inner pot. Cook on high pressure for 20 minutes, and then let the pressure release naturally.

Serves 4

Prep time
15 minutes

Pressure time
7 minutes

Release method
Natural

Bolognese Sauce

Bolognese Sauce normally simmers for hours on the stovetop, but now you can even have this rich meat sauce on a busy weeknight! Serve over your favorite pasta.

PREP INGREDIENTS

1 pound ground beef, browned, drained, and cooled

1 (28-ounce) can crushed tomatoes

2 tablespoons tomato paste

½ cup dry white wine

1 rib celery, diced

1 carrot, peeled and diced

1 small onion, chopped

4 cloves garlic, minced

2 tablespoons dehydrated minced onion

1 teaspoon dried oregano

1 teaspoon dried basil

Salt to taste

SERVING DAY INGREDIENTS

1 cup beef stock

PREP DIRECTIONS

Combine all the prep ingredients in a 1-gallon resealable freezer bag. Squeeze out the air, label, and place in a round container to freeze into shape.

SERVING DAY DIRECTIONS

Add the stock and the contents of the package to the multi-cooker inner pot. Cook on high pressure for 7 minutes, and then let the pressure release naturally.

Garlicky Beef with Pancetta and Red Wine

Serves 4

Prep time
15 minutes

Pressure time
20 minutes

Release method
Natural

Pancetta, a cured unsmoked Italian bacon, is lovely in this garlic lover's dish, but you can also substitute the same amount of ham steak. An additional tablespoon of minced garlic is stirred in at the end and cooked for just a few minutes while the sauce thickens up.

PREP INGREDIENTS

2 pounds chuck roast, cut into 1½-inch pieces

4 ounces pancetta, finely diced

1 onion, chopped

4 cloves garlic, chopped

2 carrots, chopped

2 sprigs thyme

Salt and pepper to taste

SERVING DAY INGREDIENTS

½ cup dry red wine

½ cup beef or chicken stock

1 tablespoon minced garlic

2 tablespoons cornstarch

3 tablespoons cold water

PREP DIRECTIONS

Combine all the prep ingredients in a 1-gallon resealable freezer bag. Squeeze out the air, label, and place in a round container to freeze into shape.

SERVING DAY DIRECTIONS

Add the wine, the stock, and the contents of the package to the multi-cooker inner pot. Cook on high pressure for 20 minutes, and then let the pressure release naturally. Remove the thyme sprigs. Stir in the minced garlic. Set the pot to Sauté and if there is too much liquid, let the liquid reduce, stirring occasionally. In a small bowl, mix together the cornstarch and water. Set the pot to Sauté, and stir in the cornstarch mixture until the sauce is slightly thickened.

Serves 4

Prep time
10 minutes

Pressure time
20 minutes

Release method
Natural

Short Rib Sauce

Beefy and bold, Short Rib Sauce is perfect for a cold winter's night with a glass of red wine and a fresh green salad. Serve it over your pasta of choice.

PREP INGREDIENTS

1 pound boneless beef short ribs, cut into 1-inch pieces

2 (28-ounce) cans crushed tomatoes

2 tablespoons tomato paste

1 onion, chopped

4 cloves garlic, minced

2 teaspoons dried oregano

1 teaspoon sugar

Salt and pepper to taste

SERVING DAY INGREDIENTS

½ cup dry red wine

½ cup beef stock

PREP DIRECTIONS

Combine all the prep ingredients in a 1-gallon resealable freezer bag. Squeeze out the air, label, and place in a round container to freeze into shape.

SERVING DAY DIRECTIONS

Add the wine, the stock, and the contents of the package to the multi-cooker inner pot. Cook on high pressure for 20 minutes. Let the pressure release naturally.

Serves 3 to 4

Prep time
15 minutes

Pressure time
10 minutes

Release method
Natural (10 minutes)

Pepper Steak

Pepper Steak is a Chinese-American favorite, and you'll love having it stashed away in the freezer. Serve over rice for a complete meal.

PREP INGREDIENTS

1 pound flank steak, thinly sliced

1 red bell pepper, seeded and sliced

1 green bell pepper, seeded and sliced

1 onion, halved and thinly sliced

3 cloves garlic, minced

1 teaspoon ground ginger

Salt to taste

1 teaspoon black pepper

2 tablespoons dry sherry

2 tablespoons hoisin sauce

1 tablespoon soy sauce

SERVING DAY INGREDIENTS

1 cup chicken or beef stock

2 tablespoons cornstarch

3 tablespoons cold water

1 teaspoon toasted sesame oil

PREP DIRECTIONS

Combine all the prep ingredients in a 1-gallon resealable freezer bag. Squeeze out the air, label, and place in a round container to freeze into shape.

SERVING DAY DIRECTIONS

Add the stock and the contents of the package to the multi-cooker inner pot. Cook on high pressure for 10 minutes. Let the pressure release naturally for 10 minutes, and then manually release any remaining pressure. In a small bowl, mix together the cornstarch and water. Set the pot to Sauté, and stir in the cornstarch mixture until the sauce is slightly thickened. Stir in the sesame oil.

French Dip Sandwiches

Crusty rolls, melting provolone, tender beef, and tasty au jus for dipping. What could be more fun than French Dip Sandwiches? Your family will beg you to add this one to the regular rotation!

Serves 4 to 6

Prep time
10 minutes

Pressure time
20 minutes

Release method
Natural

PREP INGREDIENTS

2 pounds chuck roast, thinly sliced

2 large onions, thinly sliced

3 cloves garlic, minced

1 tablespoon olive oil

1 tablespoon Worcestershire sauce

1 (1-ounce) packet French onion soup mix

½ teaspoon ground thyme

Salt and pepper to taste

SERVING DAY INGREDIENTS

1 cup beef stock

PREP DIRECTIONS

Combine all the prep ingredients in a 1-gallon resealable freezer bag. Squeeze out the air, label, and place in a round container to freeze into shape.

SERVING DAY DIRECTIONS

Add the stock and the contents of the package to the multi-cooker inner pot. Cook on high pressure for 20 minutes, and then let the pressure release naturally.

Steak Sandwiches

Serves 6

Prep time
10 minutes

Pressure time
20 minutes

Release method
Natural

Who needs delivery from the local pizza and sub shop when you've got steak sandwiches ready to go in the freezer? All you need for this family favorite are a pack of crusty rolls and some provolone cheese. The long cooking time will make the peppers and onions very soft, so if you prefer the peppers to be crisper, omit them from the prep bag and add them when the beef is finished, cooking for a few minutes until softened.

PREP INGREDIENTS

2 pounds blade steak, cut into 2-inch pieces (be sure to remove the center gristle in each steak)

1 (0.7-ounce) packet Italian dressing mix

1 onion, halved and sliced

2 green or red bell peppers, seeded and sliced

2 tablespoons tomato paste

Salt and pepper to taste

SERVING DAY INGREDIENTS

1 cup chicken or beef stock

6 rolls

6 slices provolone cheese

PREP DIRECTIONS

Combine all the prep ingredients in a 1-gallon resealable freezer bag. Squeeze out the air, label, and place in a round container to freeze into shape.

SERVING DAY DIRECTIONS

Add the stock and the contents of the package to the multi-cooker inner pot. Cook on high pressure for 20 minutes. Let the pressure release naturally. If desired, shred the beef with two forks. Serve on crusty rolls topped with a slice of provolone cheese. To melt the cheese, you can stick the sandwiches under the broiler for 1 to 2 minutes.

Serves 4 to 6

Prep time
15 minutes

Pressure time
10 minutes

Release method
Natural (10 minutes)

Beef and Broccoli

Thinly sliced seasoned beef and crisp-tender broccoli make Beef and Broccoli an all-time favorite. The secret is to add the broccoli at the end, so you can cook it as little or as much as you like. Serve over rice.

PREP INGREDIENTS

1½ pounds flank steak, thinly sliced into ½-inch by 2-inch pieces

1 large onion, thinly sliced

3 cloves garlic, minced

1 tablespoon minced ginger

Salt and pepper to taste

2 tablespoons soy sauce

2 tablespoons oyster sauce

1 tablespoon dry sherry

SERVING DAY INGREDIENTS

1 cup chicken stock

1 pound broccoli florets (fresh or frozen)

2 tablespoons cornstarch

3 tablespoons cold water

1 teaspoon sesame oil (optional)

PREP DIRECTIONS

Combine all the prep ingredients in a 1-gallon resealable freezer bag. Squeeze out the air, label, and place in a round container to freeze into shape.

SERVING DAY DIRECTIONS

Add the stock and the contents of the package to the multi-cooker inner pot. Cook on high pressure for 10 minutes. Let the pressure release naturally for 10 minutes, and then manually release any remaining pressure. Add the broccoli florets and cook for a few minutes until slightly tender. In a small bowl, mix together the cornstarch and water. Set the pot to Sauté, and stir in the cornstarch mixture until the sauce is slightly thickened. Add the sesame oil, if desired.

Beef Stroganoff

Change up standard beef stroganoff by using ground beef. You and your family will love this tasty version, and you'll love how quickly dinner comes together. All you need to do is cook up some egg noodles, toss them with butter, and top with the beef.

Serves 4

Prep time
20 minutes

Pressure time
8 minutes

Release method
Natural (10 minutes)

PREP INGREDIENTS

2 tablespoons olive oil, divided

1½ pounds ground beef

1 pound mushrooms, sliced

1 large onion, chopped

2 cloves garlic, minced

2 tablespoons tomato paste

½ teaspoon ground thyme

Salt and pepper to taste

1 tablespoon Worcestershire sauce

SERVING DAY INGREDIENTS

½ cup beef stock

½ cup dry red wine

1 (8-ounce) container sour cream

2 tablespoons chopped fresh parsley (optional)

PREP DIRECTIONS

Heat 1 tablespoon of the oil in a large skillet over medium heat. Add the beef and cook, breaking up large chunks with a wooden spoon. Drain the excess fat and transfer to a plate to cool. In the same pan, increase the heat to medium-high, add the remaining 1 tablespoon olive oil and the mushrooms, and cook, stirring occasionally, until golden brown. Set aside to cool. (You could use the Sauté setting in the multi-cooker, but it will be easier to cook the mushrooms in the skillet so that there's a larger surface area for them to brown.) Add the cooled meat and mushrooms, along with the remaining prep ingredients, to a 1-gallon resealable freezer bag. Squeeze out the air, label, and place in a round container to freeze into shape.

SERVING DAY DIRECTIONS

Add the stock, the red wine, and the contents of the package to the multi-cooker inner pot. Cook on high pressure for 8 minutes. Let the pressure release naturally for 10 minutes, and then manually release any remaining pressure. Stir in the sour cream and parsley (if desired).

Serves 4 to 6

Prep time
15 minutes

Pressure time
15 minutes

Release method
Natural (10 minutes)

Easy Beef Tacos

These shredded beef tacos are a nice alternative to the ground beef and seasoning packet route—and almost as simple. Serve in taco shells or on tortillas with your favorite toppings.

PREP INGREDIENTS

2 pounds chuck roast, cut into 1-inch cubes

1 onion, chopped

1 red or green bell pepper, seeded and chopped

1 (10-ounce) can diced tomatoes with green chiles

1 tablespoon olive oil

2 tablespoons chili powder

1 teaspoon smoked paprika

½ teaspoon dried oregano

Salt and pepper to taste

SERVING DAY INGREDIENTS

1 cup chicken or beef stock

PREP DIRECTIONS

Combine all the prep ingredients in a 1-gallon resealable freezer bag. Squeeze out the air, label, and place in a round container to freeze into shape.

SERVING DAY DIRECTIONS

Add the stock and the contents of the package to the multi-cooker inner pot. Cook on high pressure for 15 minutes. Let the pressure release naturally for 10 minutes, and then manually release any remaining pressure. The beef should be fork-tender. If desired, shred with two forks.

Serves 4

Prep time
15 minutes

Pressure time
20 minutes

Release method
Natural (10 minutes)

Korean Short Ribs

With just a few ordinary ingredients, these Korean Short Ribs are a breeze to whip up. Don't forget the sesame oil and sesame seeds at the end; they add a wonderfully nutty flavor. Serve over rice.

PREP INGREDIENTS

2 pounds boneless beef short ribs, cut into 1½-inch chunks

1 onion, chopped

2 carrots, peeled and sliced

4 cloves garlic, minced

1 tablespoon minced ginger

½ cup soy sauce

SERVING DAY INGREDIENTS

1 cup beef stock

1 tablespoon toasted sesame oil

2 teaspoons sesame seeds (optional)

PREP DIRECTIONS

Combine all the prep ingredients in a 1-gallon resealable freezer bag. Squeeze out the air, label, and place in a round container to freeze into shape.

SERVING DAY DIRECTIONS

Add the stock and the contents of the package to the multi-cooker inner pot. Cook on high pressure for 20 minutes. Let the pressure release naturally for 10 minutes, and then manually release any remaining pressure. Stir in the sesame oil and sprinkle with the sesame seeds, if using.

Onion-Smothered Short Ribs

Boneless short ribs aren't really ribs at all; they're actually cut from an area above the ribs. They have a good amount of marbling and are great for low, slow cooking—or pressure cooking. Here they're simply smothered in onions, beer, and French onion soup until they're fall-apart tender. Serve over mashed potatoes and don't forget to ladle on plenty of that gravy.

Serves 4 to 6

Prep time
10 minutes

Pressure time
20 minutes

Release method
Natural (10 minutes)

PREP INGREDIENTS

2 pounds boneless beef short ribs, cut into 1-inch chunks

Salt and pepper to taste

2 onions, thinly sliced

1 (10.5-ounce) can French onion soup

1 tablespoon Worcestershire sauce

SERVING DAY INGREDIENTS

1 cup beer

PREP DIRECTIONS

Season the beef chunks with salt and pepper. Add them and the remaining prep ingredients to a 1-gallon resealable freezer bag. Squeeze out the air, label, and place in a round container to freeze into shape.

SERVING DAY DIRECTIONS

Add the beer and the contents of the package to the multi-cooker inner pot. Cook on high pressure for 20 minutes. Let the pressure release naturally for 10 minutes, and then manually release any remaining pressure. Simmer the sauce for a few minutes to thicken.

Simple Sloppy Joes

Sometimes you just want a tasty sloppy Joe on a soft hamburger bun. It's nothing fancy, but always satisfying. If you like spicy food, add a little hot sauce, like sriracha, to the prep ingredients. If you want to sneak in a vegetable, add a finely chopped bell pepper to the prep bag.

Serves 4

Prep time
15 minutes

Pressure time
7 minutes

Release method
Natural (5 minutes)

PREP INGREDIENTS

1½ pounds ground beef or turkey, browned and cooled

1 small onion, chopped

2 cloves garlic, chopped

¾ cup ketchup

1 tablespoon Worcestershire sauce

1 tablespoon yellow or Dijon mustard

1 tablespoon packed brown sugar

Salt to taste

SERVING DAY INGREDIENTS

1 cup chicken stock

PREP DIRECTIONS

Combine all the prep ingredients in a 1-gallon resealable freezer bag. Squeeze out the air, label, and place in a round container to freeze into shape.

SERVING DAY DIRECTIONS

Add the stock and the contents of the package to the multi-cooker inner pot. Cook on high pressure for 7 minutes. Let the pressure release naturally for 5 minutes, and then manually release any remaining pressure. Simmer to thicken the sauce if desired. Serve on hamburger buns.

Serves 4

Prep time
15 minutes

Pressure time
20 minutes

Release method
Natural (10 minutes)

Swiss Steak

There are many variations of Swiss steak. Most of them involve a simple braise of beef in a tomato or mushroom sauce. With this freezer meal, you'll be surprised at how something so simple could be so satisfying. Serve over mashed potatoes for a lick-the-plate-clean dinner.

PREP INGREDIENTS

2 pounds blade steak, cut into 2-inch chunks

1 (0.7-ounce) packet Italian dressing mix

1 onion, chopped

3 cloves garlic, minced

1 (14.5-ounce) can diced tomatoes

2 tablespoons tomato paste

1 tablespoon soy sauce

1 tablespoon vinegar (preferably red wine vinegar)

½ teaspoon black pepper

SERVING DAY INGREDIENTS

1 cup chicken or beef stock
Chopped fresh parsley, for garnish (optional)

PREP DIRECTIONS

Combine all the prep ingredients in a 1-gallon resealable freezer bag. Squeeze out the air, label, and place in a round container to freeze into shape.

SERVING DAY DIRECTIONS

Add the stock and the contents of the package to the multi-cooker inner pot. Cook on high pressure for 20 minutes. Let the pressure release naturally for 10 minutes, and then manually release any remaining pressure. Sprinkle with chopped fresh parsley, if desired.

Classic Italian Meatballs

Win at spaghetti night with these Classic Italian Meatballs. The meatballs are individually frozen and then cooked together with a jar of sauce and some water. All you need to do is boil the spaghetti on the stovetop.

Serves 4 to 6

Prep time
20 minutes

Pressure time
6 minutes

Release method
Natural (10 minutes)

PREP INGREDIENTS

1½ pounds ground beef

2 tablespoons minced onion

2 cloves garlic, minced

1 large egg, beaten

½ cup breadcrumbs

¼ cup minced fresh parsley

1 teaspoon salt

¼ teaspoon ground pepper

SERVING DAY INGREDIENTS

1½ cups water

1 (25-ounce) jar tomato sauce

PREP DIRECTIONS

In a large bowl, mix together all of the prep ingredients. Roll the mixture into 1½-inch balls, place on a parchment paper–lined baking sheet, and freeze. Once the meatballs are completely frozen, transfer them to a 1-gallon resealable freezer bag. Squeeze out the air, label, and place in a round container to freeze into shape.

SERVING DAY DIRECTIONS

Add the water, the tomato sauce, and the meatballs to the inner pot. Cook on high pressure for 6 minutes. Let the pressure release naturally for 10 minutes, and then manually release any remaining pressure.

Serves 4

Prep time
10 minutes

Pressure time
8 minutes

Release method
Natural (10 minutes)

Salisbury Steak Meatballs

For a delicious bit of retro fun, try these Salisbury Steak Meatballs, which you can throw together with store-bought meatballs and a few other ingredients. Everyone will love them! They're great with mashed potatoes or buttered noodles.

PREP INGREDIENTS

1 (2-pound) bag fully cooked
frozen meatballs

1 large onion, thinly sliced

½ cup dry white wine

1 tablespoon tomato paste

½ teaspoon dried thyme

1 (0.87-ounce) package brown gravy mix

SERVING DAY INGREDIENTS

1 cup water

8 ounces mushrooms, sliced (optional)

2 tablespoons chopped fresh parsley

2 tablespoons cornstarch (optional)

3 tablespoons cold water (optional)

PREP DIRECTIONS

Combine all the prep ingredients in a 1-gallon resealable freezer bag. Squeeze out the air, label, and place in a round container to freeze into shape.

SERVING DAY DIRECTIONS

Add the water and the contents of the package to the multi-cooker inner pot. Cook on high pressure for 8 minutes. Let the pressure release naturally for 10 minutes, and then manually release any remaining pressure. Add the mushrooms, if desired, and the parsley. Set the pot to Sauté and cook until the mushrooms are slightly tender. If the sauce is too thin, in a small bowl, stir together the cornstarch and water. Set the pot to Sauté, and stir in the cornstarch mixture until the sauce is slightly thickened.

Picadillo

If you're not familiar with Picadillo, it's a spiced ground meat dish popular throughout Latin America in various iterations. It may soon be a requested favorite, even with the picky eaters in your house!

Serves 4 to 6

Prep time
15 minutes

Pressure time
7 minutes

Release method
Natural (5 minutes)

PREP INGREDIENTS

1 pound ground beef, browned, drained, and cooled

1 pound fresh chorizo sausage, casing removed, browned, drained, and cooled

1 onion, chopped

3 cloves garlic, minced

1 cup canned diced tomatoes, drained

1 tablespoon vinegar

½ cup coarsely chopped pimento-stuffed green olives or black olives

⅓ cup raisins (optional)

½ teaspoon dried oregano

½ teaspoon ground cumin

Salt and pepper to taste

SERVING DAY INGREDIENTS

1 cup chicken or beef stock

2 tablespoons cornstarch (optional)

3 tablespoons cold water (optional)

PREP DIRECTIONS

Combine all the prep ingredients in a 1-gallon resealable freezer bag. Squeeze out the air, label, and place in a round container to freeze into shape.

SERVING DAY DIRECTIONS

Add the stock and the contents of the package to the multi-cooker inner pot. Cook on high pressure for 7 minutes. Let the pressure release naturally for 5 minutes, and then manually release the pressure. If the sauce is too thin, in a small bowl, stir together the cornstarch and water. Set the pot to Sauté, and stir in the cornstarch mixture until the sauce is slightly thickened.

Serves 4

Prep time
15 minutes

Pressure time
7 minutes

Release method
Natural (10 minutes)

Chili Mac

The ultimate all-in-one meal, Chili Mac checks all the right boxes. It's a cheesy, meaty pasta dish sure to please the young (and the young at heart) in your family.

PREP INGREDIENTS

1 pound ground beef, browned and cooled

1 onion, chopped

3 cloves garlic, minced

1 (14.5-ounce) can diced tomatoes

1 (4.5-ounce) can green chiles

1 (15.5-ounce) can kidney beans, drained and rinsed

2 tablespoons chili powder

Salt and pepper to taste

SERVING DAY INGREDIENTS

1 cup chicken or beef stock

2 cups dried macaroni

1 cup shredded cheese (such as cheddar, Monterey Jack, or pepper Jack)

¼ cup chopped fresh cilantro

PREP DIRECTIONS

Combine all the prep ingredients in a 1-gallon resealable freezer bag. Squeeze out the air, label, and place in a round container to freeze into shape.

SERVING DAY DIRECTIONS

Add the stock and the contents of the package to the multi-cooker inner pot. Cook on high pressure for 7 minutes. Let the pressure release naturally for 10 minutes, and then manually release any remaining pressure. Meanwhile, on the stovetop, bring a large pot of salted water to a boil, add the macaroni, and cook, stirring occasionally, until tender. Drain, and stir into the chili, along with the cheese and cilantro.

Chipotle Carnitas

Skip the line at the taco shop and just pull these tasty carnitas—seasoned with citrus, oregano, garlic, and chipotle—from the freezer. Warm up some corn tortillas and serve them topped with sliced radishes, chopped cilantro, and a squeeze of lime juice.

Serves 4

Prep time
15 minutes

Pressure time
15 minutes

Release method
Natural

PREP INGREDIENTS

2 pounds pork shoulder or butt, cut into 1-inch cubes

4 cloves garlic, minced

1 chopped canned chile in adodo

2 teaspoons dried oregano

1½ teaspoons salt

1 teaspoon black pepper

¼ cup orange juice

SERVING DAY INGREDIENTS

1 cup chicken or beef stock

PREP DIRECTIONS

Combine all the prep ingredients in a 1-gallon resealable freezer bag. Squeeze out the air, label, and place in a round container to freeze into shape.

SERVING DAY DIRECTIONS

Add the stock and the contents of the package to the multi-cooker inner pot. Cook on high pressure for 15 minutes. Let the pressure release naturally. When cool enough to handle, shred the pork with two forks. If you prefer your carnitas crispy, transfer the meat to a large skillet. Cook over medium-high heat, stirring regularly, until the edges are crispy and browned in spots. Top with a little of the sauce if desired.

Serves 4

Prep time
15 minutes

Pressure time
20 minutes

Release method
Natural (10 minutes)

Apple and Cranberry Pork Loin

Enjoy the flavors of fall with Apple and Cranberry Pork Loin. When selecting the pork, be sure to choose pork loin, not the small tenderloin, which is too lean for this recipe.

PREP INGREDIENTS

2 pounds pork loin, cut into 1-inch cubes

3 cups cubed butternut squash

½ onion, chopped

⅓ cup dried cranberries

½ teaspoon dried sage

¼ teaspoon dried rosemary

Salt and pepper to taste

SERVING DAY INGREDIENTS

1 cup apple cider

2 tablespoons cornstarch (optional)

2 tablespoons cold water (optional)

2 tablespoons unsalted butter

PREP DIRECTIONS

Combine all the prep ingredients in a 1-gallon resealable freezer bag. Squeeze out the air, label, and place in a round container to freeze into shape.

SERVING DAY DIRECTIONS

Add the apple cider and the contents of the package to the multi-cooker inner pot. Cook on high pressure for 20 minutes. Let the pressure release naturally for 10 minutes, and then manually release any remaining pressure. If the sauce is too thin, in a small bowl, mix together the cornstarch and water. Set the pot to Sauté, and stir in the cornstarch mixture until the sauce is slightly thickened. Stir in the butter until melted. Serve the sauce over the pork.

Maple Pork with Sauerkraut and Apples

Serves 4 to 6

Prep time
15 minutes

Pressure time
20 minutes

Release method
Natural (10 minutes)

Pork and sauerkraut is a traditional combination, and in Pennsylvania, it's considered good luck to eat it on New Year's Day. This version adds apple and maple syrup for a tasty twist on the original. Sauerkraut has a lot of sodium, so don't add too much salt to the prep ingredients. Taste the finished dish and add as needed.

PREP INGREDIENTS

2 pounds pork loin or pork shoulder, cut into 1-inch chunks

1 apple, peeled and diced

1 onion, chopped

3 tablespoons maple syrup

Salt and pepper to taste

SERVING DAY INGREDIENTS

1 cup chicken stock

1 (14.5-ounce) container sauerkraut

2 tablespoons unsalted butter

Salt and pepper to taste

PREP DIRECTIONS

Combine all the prep ingredients in a 1-gallon resealable freezer bag. Squeeze out the air, label, and place in a round container to freeze into shape.

SERVING DAY DIRECTIONS

Add the stock and the contents of the package to the multi-cooker inner pot. Cook on high pressure for 20 minutes. Let the pressure release naturally for 10 minutes, and then manually release any remaining pressure. Stir in the sauerkraut and butter until melted. Season to taste with salt and pepper.

Serves 4

Prep time
15 minutes

Pressure time
15 minutes

Release method
Natural (15 minutes)

Caribbean-Spiced Pork

Channel the Caribbean with this pork shoulder seasoned with ginger, allspice, and thyme. It's delicious served over rice and even better with some plantain chips and a mango-avocado salsa on the side!

PREP INGREDIENTS

2 pounds pork shoulder or butt, cut into 1-inch cubes

1 onion, chopped

3 cloves garlic, chopped

1 teaspoon ground ginger

1 teaspoon ground allspice

1 teaspoon ground thyme

1 teaspoon salt

½ cup orange juice

SERVING DAY INGREDIENTS

1 cup chicken or beef stock

PREP DIRECTIONS

Combine all the prep ingredients in a 1-gallon resealable freezer bag. Squeeze out the air, label, and place in a round container to freeze into shape.

SERVING DAY DIRECTIONS

Add the stock and the contents of the package to the multi-cooker inner pot. Cook on high pressure for 15 minutes. Let the pressure release naturally. The pork should be fork-tender. Once cool enough to handle, shred the pork with two forks.

Provençal Pork with White Beans

Serves 4 to 6

Prep time
15 minutes

Pressure time
15 minutes

Release method
Natural

French-style pork and beans? Absolutely. In France, they tend to prefer white beans like flageolet with meats like pork and lamb, but those can be hard to find, so just use cannellini beans. Herbes de Provence is a blend that often contains basil, rosemary, fennel, rosemary, thyme, sage, and other herbs. You can usually find it in the spice aisle of the supermarket. If you can't find it, you could even use a poultry seasoning, although the flavor wouldn't be quite the same.

PREP INGREDIENTS

1½ pounds boneless pork shoulder, cut into 1-inch chunks

1 onion, chopped

1 rib celery, chopped

2 carrots, peeled and chopped

5 cloves garlic, minced

2 teaspoons herbes de Provence

1 bay leaf

Salt and pepper to taste

SERVING DAY INGREDIENTS

½ cup dry white wine

½ cup chicken stock

1 (15.5-ounce) can cannellini beans, drained and rinsed

Chopped fresh parsley, for garnish (optional)

PREP DIRECTIONS

Combine all the prep ingredients in a 1-gallon resealable freezer bag. Squeeze out the air, label, and place in a round container to freeze into shape.

SERVING DAY DIRECTIONS

Add the wine, the stock, and the contents of the package to the multi-cooker inner pot. Cook on high pressure for 15 minutes. Let the pressure release naturally. The pork should be fork-tender and shred easily. Set the pot to Sauté. Stir in the beans and cook until heated through. If desired, garnish with chopped parsley.

Serves 4

Prep time
10 minutes

Pressure time
15 minutes

Release method
Natural

Braised Pork with Mustard and Sour Cream Sauce

For a casual French-inspired dinner that takes little effort, try tender Braised Pork with Mustard and Sour Cream Sauce. Serve with fingerling potatoes and a salad for a little weeknight ooh-la-la.

PREP INGREDIENTS

2 pounds pork shoulder, cut into 1-inch cubes

2 shallots, chopped

2 tablespoon grainy mustard

2 teaspoons Dijon mustard

Salt and pepper to taste

SERVING DAY INGREDIENTS

1 cup chicken or beef stock

2 tablespoons cornstarch

3 tablespoons cold water

½ cup sour cream

PREP DIRECTIONS

Combine all the prep ingredients in a 1-gallon resealable freezer bag. Squeeze out the air, label, and place in a round container to freeze into shape.

SERVING DAY DIRECTIONS

Add the stock and the contents of the package to the multi-cooker inner pot. Cook on high pressure for 15 minutes. Let the pressure release naturally. The pork should be fork-tender. In a small bowl, stir together the cornstarch and water. Set the pot to Sauté, and stir in the cornstarch mixture until the sauce is slightly thickened. Stir in the sour cream.

Kielbasa, Black-Eyed Pea, and Butternut Squash Stew

Serves 4

Prep time
15 minutes

Pressure time
7 minutes

Release method
Natural (10 minutes)

With sweet butternut squash, smoked kielbasa, and hearty black-eyed peas, this well-balanced stew is a one-pot wonder.

PREP INGREDIENTS

1 (15.5-ounce) can black-eyed peas, drained and rinsed

1 pound kielbasa sausage, sliced

3 cups cubed butternut squash

1 onion, chopped

1 rib celery, chopped

1 teaspoon paprika

2 bay leaves

2 tablespoons tomato paste

Salt and pepper to taste

SERVING DAY INGREDIENTS

1 cup chicken or beef stock

PREP DIRECTIONS

Combine all the prep ingredients in a 1-gallon resealable freezer bag. Squeeze out the air, label, and place in a round container to freeze into shape.

SERVING DAY DIRECTIONS

Add the stock and the contents of the package to the multi-cooker inner pot. Cook on high pressure for 7 minutes. Let the pressure release naturally for 10 minutes, and then manually release any remaining pressure.

Serves 4 to 6

Prep time
15 minutes

Pressure time
15 minutes

Release method
Natural

Pork and Hominy Stew

Hominy, a type of dried corn, is one of the first foods Native Americans gave to the colonists. When hominy is ground, it becomes grits or masa (which is used to make tortillas). In its whole form it is often used in the Mexican stew posole, which means "hominy" in Spanish. You can usually find canned hominy near the canned beans or near other Latin American products in the supermarket. Serve topped with your choice of chopped radishes, cubed avocado, chopped onion, and lime wedges.

PREP INGREDIENTS

1 pound pork shoulder, cut into 1-inch chunks

1 onion, chopped

3 cloves garlic, chopped

1 jalapeño, chopped (seeded for less heat, if desired)

1 (15-ounce) can red enchilada sauce

1 (4.5-ounce) can green chiles

1 teaspoon paprika

Salt to taste

SERVING DAY INGREDIENTS

2 cups chicken or beef stock

1 (28-ounce) can hominy, drained and rinsed

¼ cup chopped fresh cilantro

PREP DIRECTIONS

Combine all the prep ingredients in a 1-gallon resealable freezer bag. Squeeze out the air, label, and place in a round container to freeze into shape.

SERVING DAY DIRECTIONS

Add the stock and the contents of the package to the multi-cooker inner pot. Cook on high pressure for 15 minutes. Let the pressure release naturally. The pork should be fork-tender and shred easily. Using a slotted spoon, remove the pork to a bowl and shred with two forks. Set the pot to Sauté and stir in the hominy. Return the pork to the pot. Cook until the hominy is heated through and the flavors have melded, about 5 minutes. Stir in the cilantro.

Street Food Tacos

Street Food Tacos are inspired by tacos al pastor, a Central Mexican-style taco, filled with pineapple- and chile-spiked meat that's shaved off a spit. Here, tender chunks of pork shoulder meld with those same flavors for a comforting meal. The pineapple dissolves into the finished dish, becoming just a sweet and fruity note balancing out the richness of the pork. If you're a fan of the pork-pineapple combination, add a few chunks of fresh (or even grilled) pineapple on the taco. Serve on warmed corn tortillas with any or all of these toppings: chopped onion, cilantro, avocado, sour cream, and lime juice.

Serves 4 to 6

Prep time
15 minutes

Pressure time
25 minutes

Release method
Natural (10 minutes)

PREP INGREDIENTS

2 pounds pork shoulder, cut into 1-inch cubes

½ onion, chopped

3 cloves garlic, crushed

¼ cup crushed canned pineapple

2 tablespoons ancho chile powder

2 teaspoons chopped canned chipotle pepper in adobo

½ teaspoon ground cumin

½ teaspoon dried oregano

1 tablespoon vinegar

Salt to taste

SERVING DAY INGREDIENTS

1 cup chicken stock

PREP DIRECTIONS

Combine all the prep ingredients in a 1-gallon resealable freezer bag. Squeeze out the air, label, and place in a round container to freeze into shape.

SERVING DAY DIRECTIONS

Add the stock and the contents of the package to the multi-cooker inner pot. Cook on high pressure for 25 minutes. Let the pressure release naturally for 10 minutes, and then manually release any remaining pressure. Using a slotted spoon, transfer the pork to a bowl and shred with two forks. Meanwhile, turn the pot to Sauté and reduce the liquid, stirring frequently, until it's like a glaze, about 10 minutes. Add some of the sauce to the pork and toss to coat.

Serves 4

Prep time
15 minutes

Pressure time
7 minutes

Release method
Natural

Italian Sausage Stew

Italian Sausage Stew is a delicious combination of hearty vegetables, chickpeas, and seasoned chunks of sausage. It's a complete meal in a bowl! Just sprinkle with some Parmesan cheese and serve with crusty Italian bread and butter.

PREP INGREDIENTS

½ pound sweet or hot Italian sausage, casings removed, browned and cooled to room temperature

1 onion, chopped

1 carrot, chopped

1 red bell pepper, seeded and chopped

1 rib celery, chopped

1 tablespoon minced garlic

1 cup canned diced tomatoes, drained

1 (15.5-ounce) can chickpeas, drained and rinsed

Salt and pepper to taste

SERVING DAY INGREDIENTS

2 cups chicken or beef stock

PREP DIRECTIONS

Combine all the prep ingredients in a 1-gallon resealable freezer bag. Squeeze out the air, label, and place in a round container to freeze into shape.

SERVING DAY DIRECTIONS

Add the stock and the contents of the package to the multi-cooker inner pot. Cook on high pressure for 7 minutes, and then let the pressure release naturally.

Sausage Lasagna

You'll love the streamlined prep of this Sausage Lasagna. Instead of layering the ricotta, Parmesan, and mozzarella individually, they're all mixed together in one bowl and layered with the sauce, meat, and noodles. Suddenly, making a lasagna doesn't seem so daunting after all! Plus, there's nothing better than knowing you have a lasagna in the freezer.

Serves 4 to 6

Prep time
25 minutes

Pressure time
20 minutes

Release method
Natural (10 minutes)

PREP INGREDIENTS

1 egg, lightly beaten

8 ounces shredded mozzarella cheese, divided

1 (16-ounce) container ricotta cheese

½ cup grated Parmesan cheese

Pinch ground nutmeg (optional)

Salt and pepper to taste

1 (25-ounce) jar tomato sauce (optional)

1 (9-ounce) package no-boil lasagna noodles (optional)

1 pound bulk Italian sausage meat (sweet or hot), browned and cooled

SERVING DAY INGREDIENTS

1½ cups water

PREP DIRECTIONS

In a medium bowl, stir together the egg, two-thirds of the mozzarella, ricotta, Parmesan, nutmeg (if using), and salt and pepper. Spread a thin layer of sauce over the bottom of a 7-inch springform pan. Break up the uncooked lasagna noodles and place them in a single layer on the bottom of the pan. Spread a layer of cooled sausage, then a layer of the cheese mixture, then a layer of sauce. Top with another layer of noodles broken to fit. Continue layering, ending with a final layer of noodles and sauce. Top with the remaining one-third mozzarella cheese. Cover tightly with aluminum foil and freeze.

SERVING DAY DIRECTIONS

Thaw the lasagna completely in the refrigerator. Add the water and the trivet to the bottom of the multi-cooker. Using a foil sling, gently lower the covered lasagna onto the trivet. Tuck in the foil ends and cook on high pressure for 20 minutes. Let the pressure release naturally for 10 minutes, and then manually release any remaining pressure. Let rest for 15 minutes before releasing from the springform pan and slicing.

Serves 4 to 6

Prep time
10 minutes

Pressure time
10 minutes

Release method
Natural

Sausage and Lentil Stew

Traditionally, this recipe uses links of Italian sausage, but here we mix things up a bit and use smoky kielbasa, which browns up in just a few minutes on serving day. If you want to use Italian sausage, you can cook the bulk meat in advance and include it in your freezer bag. See the headnote on page 25 for tips on preparing the lentils.

PREP INGREDIENTS

1 cup dried brown lentils, picked over for debris and rinsed

1 onion, chopped

3 cloves garlic, minced

¼ cup dry red wine

Salt and pepper to taste

SERVING DAY INGREDIENTS

1 cup chicken stock

1 pound kielbasa sausage, sliced into ½-inch rounds

PREP DIRECTIONS

Add the lentils to the multi-cooker along with enough water to cover by about an inch. Lock the lid and cook on high pressure for 10 minutes. Let the pressure release naturally and drain the lentils. Once cooled, add them to a 1-gallon resealable plastic bag along with the remaining prep ingredients. Squeeze out the air, label, and place in a round container to freeze into shape.

SERVING DAY DIRECTIONS

Add the stock and the contents of the package to the multi-cooker inner pot. Cook on high pressure for 5 minutes. Let the pressure release naturally for 5 minutes, and then manually release any remaining pressure. Meanwhile, in a nonstick skillet over medium heat, brown the kielbasa slices on both sides, about 5 minutes. Top the stew with the browned sausage.

Fish
& Seafood

Serves 4

Prep time
5 minutes

Pressure time
2 minutes

Release method
Manual

Lemon-Dill Cod

Everyone needs a basic fish recipe, and while the multi-cooker isn't always the best place to cook something delicate like fish, frozen fish works in your favor because it's less likely to be overcooked. Other thick white fish would work well in the recipe, too. You can even pick up frozen fillets from the supermarket, keep them in the freezer, and then just add the toppings on serving day.

PREP INGREDIENTS

4 (5- to 6-ounce) fillets fresh cod

Salt and pepper to taste

2 tablespoons minced fresh dill leaves

4 tablespoons unsalted butter, sliced

4 thin slices lemon

SERVING DAY INGREDIENTS

1 cup water

PREP DIRECTIONS

Season each fillet with salt and pepper. Top each fillet with dill, 1 tablespoon butter, and 1 slice lemon. Place each piece on a parchment paper–lined sheet of aluminum foil. Wrap individually and place in a 1-gallon resealable freezer bag. Squeeze out the air, label, and freeze.

SERVING DAY DIRECTIONS

Add the water and the trivet to the bottom of the multi-cooker. Place a piece of foil on top of the trivet to catch any drippings. Unwrap the fish and place the fillets on top of the trivet in a single layer (as flat as possible). Cook on low pressure for 2 minutes. Manually release the pressure. Check for doneness.

Mediterranean Cod

Jazz up some simple cod with sun-dried tomatoes, olives, and oregano! With just a handful of ingredients, you can serve this warm, satisfying meal in minutes any day of the week.

Serves 4

Prep time
5 minutes

Pressure time
2 minutes

Release method
Manual

PREP INGREDIENTS

4 (5- to 6-ounce) fillets fresh cod

Salt and pepper to taste

2 teaspoons chopped fresh oregano or ½ teaspoon dried oregano

4 tablespoons chopped sun-dried tomatoes in oil

4 tablespoons sliced pitted kalamata olives

4 teaspoons extra-virgin olive oil

SERVING DAY INGREDIENTS

1 cup water

Lemon wedges, for serving (optional)

PREP DIRECTIONS

Season each fillet with salt, pepper, and oregano. Top each fillet with 1 tablespoon sun-dried tomatoes and 1 tablespoon kalamata olives. Drizzle with each the 1 teaspoon olive oil. Place each piece on a parchment paper-lined sheet of aluminum foil. Wrap individually and place in a 1-gallon resealable freezer bag. Squeeze out the air, label, and freeze.

SERVING DAY DIRECTIONS

Add the water and the trivet to the bottom of the multi-cooker. Place a piece of foil on top of the trivet to catch any drippings. Unwrap the fish and place the fillets on top of the trivet in a single layer (as flat as possible). Cook on low pressure for 2 minutes. Manually release the pressure. Check for doneness. If desired, serve with lemon wedges.

Pesto Salmon

Pesto Salmon is so simple that you don't even need to prep it ahead of time! As long as you have frozen fish and pesto on hand, you have dinner.

Serves 4

Prep time
5 minutes

Pressure time
2 minutes

Release method
Manual

PREP INGREDIENTS

4 (5- to 6-ounce) fresh salmon fillets, preferably wild-caught

¼ to ⅓ cup homemade or store-bought pesto

SERVING DAY INGREDIENTS

1 cup water

Lemon wedges, for serving

PREP DIRECTIONS

Coat the salmon fillets with 1 tablespoon or so of the pesto. Place each piece on a parchment paper–lined sheet of aluminum foil. Wrap each piece individually and place in a 1-gallon resealable freezer bag. Squeeze out the air, label, and freeze.

SERVING DAY DIRECTIONS

Add the water and the trivet to the bottom of the multi-cooker. Place a piece of foil on top of the trivet to catch any drippings. Unwrap the fish and place the fillets on top of the trivet in a single layer (as flat as possible). Cook on low pressure for 2 minutes, and then manually release the pressure. Check for doneness. Spoon any extra pesto on top of the fish and serve with lemon wedges.

Serves 4 to 6

Prep time
10 minutes

Pressure time
7 minutes

Release method
Natural (5 minutes)

Shrimp and Sausage Jambalaya

Jambalaya is a Louisiana dish with French and Spanish roots. There are many iterations, but this one uses andouille sausage and shrimp. To keep the meal freezer friendly, the rice is cooked up separately on serving day. You can either serve the jambalaya on top of the rice or toss it all together.

PREP INGREDIENTS

1 pound cooked andouille or smoked sausage, cut into 1-inch-thick slices

1 onion, chopped

1 green bell pepper, seeded and chopped

2 teaspoons Cajun seasoning

1 (8-ounce) can tomato sauce

1 tablespoon Worcestershire or soy sauce

Salt and pepper to taste

SERVING DAY INGREDIENTS

1 cup chicken stock

1 pound fresh shrimp, peeled and deveined

2 cups rice, cooked according to package directions

PREP DIRECTIONS

Combine all the prep ingredients in a 1-gallon resealable freezer bag. Squeeze out the air, label, and place in a round container to freeze into shape.

SERVING DAY DIRECTIONS

Add the stock and the contents of the package to the multi-cooker inner pot. Cook on high pressure for 7 minutes. Let the pressure release naturally for 5 minutes, and then manually release any remaining pressure. Stir in the shrimp, replace the lid on the pot but do not lock it, and let the shrimp cook in the residual heat, about 4 minutes. When cooked through, serve over the rice, or stir the rice into the pot and serve from there.

Shrimp Scampi

Shrimp Scampi is a delicious treat you might only have thought of ordering at a restaurant, but it's so simple to make at home in the multi-cooker—any night of the week. The key is to use frozen shrimp, which helps prevent overcooking. Serve over pasta.

Serves 4

Prep time
5 minutes

Pressure time
1 minute

Release method
Manual

PREP INGREDIENTS

2 pounds frozen peeled and deveined shrimp

5 cloves garlic, minced

¼ cup minced fresh parsley

Salt and pepper to taste

¼ cup dry white wine

SERVING DAY INGREDIENTS

1 cup chicken stock

1 tablespoon lemon juice

4 tablespoons unsalted butter

PREP DIRECTIONS

Keep the shrimp frozen separately from the other ingredients. Combine the remaining prep ingredients in a small resealable freezer bag. Squeeze out the air, label, and freeze.

SERVING DAY DIRECTIONS

Add the stock, the shrimp, and the contents of the package to the multi-cooker inner pot. Cook on high pressure for 1 minute. Manually release the pressure. Using a slotted spoon, transfer the shrimp to a bowl. Simmer the sauce until slightly thickened, 2 to 3 minutes, and then stir in the lemon juice and butter. Toss the shrimp with the sauce.

Serves 4

Prep time
10 minutes

Pressure time
2 minutes

Release method
Manual

Herb-Crusted Salmon

Delicious and good for you too, Herb-Crusted Salmon goes from frozen to finished in a flash. You can use other tender herbs—such as dill, chives, and mint—depending on what's in season and what you have around.

PREP INGREDIENTS

2 cloves garlic, minced

2 tablespoons olive oil

1 tablespoon Dijon mustard

2 tablespoons chopped parsley

1 teaspoon chopped tarragon

Salt and black pepper to taste

4 (5- to 6-ounce) fresh salmon fillets, preferably wild-caught

SERVING DAY INGREDIENTS

1 cup water

PREP DIRECTIONS

In a small bowl, mix together the garlic, olive oil, mustard, parsley, and tarragon. Season to taste with salt and pepper. Spread the mixture evenly over the fillets. Place each piece on a parchment paper-lined sheet of aluminum foil. Wrap each piece individually and place in a 1-gallon resealable freezer bag. Squeeze out the air, label, and freeze.

SERVING DAY DIRECTIONS

Add the water and the trivet to the bottom of the multi-cooker. Place a piece of foil on top of the trivet to catch any drippings. Unwrap the fish and place the fillets on top of the trivet in a single layer (as flat as possible). Cook on low pressure for 2 minutes. Manually release the pressure. Check for doneness.

MEASUREMENT

CUP	OUNCES	MILLILITERS	TABLESPOONS
8 cup	64 oz	1895 ml	128
6 cup	48 oz	1420 ml	96
5 cup	40 oz	1180 ml	80
4 cup	32 oz	960 ml	64
2 cup	16 oz	480 ml	32
1 cup	8 oz	240 ml	16
3/4 cup	6 oz	177 ml	12
2/3 cup	5 oz	158 ml	11
1/2 cup	4 oz	118 ml	8
3/8 cup	3 oz	90 ml	6
1/3 cup	2.5 oz	79 ml	5.5
1/4 cup	2 oz	59 ml	4
1/8 cup	1 oz	30 ml	3
1/16 cup	1/2 oz	15 ml	1

TEMPERATURE

FAHRENHEIT	CELSIUS
100 °F	37 °C
150 °F	65 °C
200 °F	93 °C
250 °F	121 °C
300 °F	150 °C
325 °F	160 °C
350 °F	180 °C
375 °F	190 °C
400 °F	200 °C
425 °F	220 °C
450 °F	230 °C
500 °F	260 °C
525 °F	274 °C
550 °F	288 °C

WEIGHT

IMPERIAL	METRIC
1/2 oz	15 g
1 oz	29 g
2 oz	57 g
3 oz	85 g
4 oz	113 g
5 oz	141 g
6 oz	170 g
8 oz	227 g
10 oz	283 g
12 oz	340 g
13 oz	369 g
14 oz	397 g
15 oz	425 g
1 lb	453 g

Index

LOOK FOR THESE OTHER COOKBOOKS BY

ELLA SANDERS!

SUPER FAST INSTANT POT PRESSURE COOKER COOKBOOK
100 EASY RECIPES FOR EVERY MULTI-COOKER
HEATHER RODINO & ELLA SANDERS

THE BEST **AIR FRYER RECIPES** ON THE PLANET
OVER 125 EASY, FOOLPROOF FRIED FAVORITES WITHOUT ALL THE FAT
ELLA SANDERS

COPPER Magic!
NO-FAIL RECIPES FOR THE Revolutionary New Nonstick Cookware
ELLA SANDERS

COPPER Magic! **ONE-POT MEALS**
NO-FUSS RECIPES FOR THE REVOLUTIONARY NEW NONSTICK COOKWARE
ELLA SANDERS
Author of THE ULTIMATE INSTANT POT COOKBOOK

THE ULTIMATE **INSTANT POT** PRESSURE COOKER COOKBOOK
200 EASY FOOLPROOF RECIPES
ELLA SANDERS

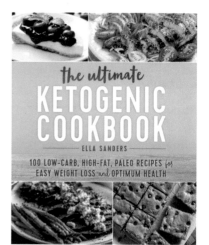

the ultimate **KETOGENIC COOKBOOK**
ELLA SANDERS
100 LOW-CARB, HIGH-FAT, PALEO RECIPES for EASY WEIGHT LOSS and OPTIMUM HEALTH